WACO-McLENNAN
1717 AUS
WACO TX 76701

MW00848529

LAST
TRAIN
to
TEXAS

LAST TRAIN to TEXAS

My Railroad Odyssey

FRED W. FRAILEY

INDIANA UNIVERSITY PRESS

This book is a publication of

Indiana University Press
Office of Scholarly Publishing
Herman B Wells Library 350
1320 East 10th Street
Bloomington, Indiana 47405 USA

iupress.indiana.edu

Manufactured in the United States of America

Library of Congress Cataloging-in-Publication Data

Names: Frailey, Fred W., author.
Title: Last train to Texas : my railroad odyssey / Fred W. Frailey.
Other titles: Railroads past and present.
Description: Bloomington : Indiana University Press, 2020. | Series:
   Railroads past and present
Identifiers: LCCN 2019033925 (print) | LCCN 2019033926 (ebook) | ISBN
   9780253045249 (hardback) | ISBN 9780253045270 (ebook)
Subjects: LCSH: Frailey, Fred W.—Travel. | Railroad travel—Anecdotes.
Classification: LCC HE1038.F73 L388 2020 (print) | LCC HE1038.F73 (ebook)
   | DDC 385.0973—dc23
LC record available at https://lccn.loc.gov/2019033925
LC ebook record available at https://lccn.loc.gov/2019033926

1 2 3 4 5   25 24 23 22 21 20

CONTENTS

FOREWORD

FRED FRAILEY AND RAILROADS HAVE been inextricably linked for more than 40 years—60 if you count his apprenticeship hanging around railroad depots and yards as a youngster. It's a good thing, too, because for those of us who love this industry, Fred has been a constant source of in- depth analysis, insight, and stories about the people who make our business work, all of which have served to illuminate so much of the change we've seen during his tenure as a writer.

Railroads are a big business, requiring enormous sums of capital (frequently as much as 18–20 percent or so of annual revenue). They use huge locomotives and rolling stock that move over vast distances to do the jobs for which they're required, and they demand extremely skilled professionals to move the trains over the road and to manage the far-flung systems. Making these systems work well is a big job.

Fred has brought together a unique set of skills and talent to keep us, his readers, abreast of the latest changes in the industry. In addition to the sheer size of the industry, it is continually changing, evolving, and redefining itself, often in response to changing regulations, management whims, and market conditions. Fred has been at the forefront of allowing his readers to follow and even to anticipate changes, through his articles, columns, and blogs.

In some ways, though, Fred Frailey is a bit of an enigma. For many of us who grew up in and around the industry, our dream was to work for a railroad and bring energy, vision, and passion into our chosen line of work. Fred, on the other hand, while showing an early passion for railroading, was also influenced by his father, a newspaperman in the old tradition of being ready to find the big story, ask hard and probing questions, and then take his efforts to the public in his own writing style. In that respect, Fred is the proverbial chip off the old block. He has effectively married his passion for railroads and his considerable writing gifts to become one of the United States' foremost railroad storytellers.

Since Fred began his professional writing career, he observed dramatic changes in the industry, including the passage of the landmark Staggers Act and the creation of Conrail at a time when many observers believed eastern railroads could have been nationalized. He also had the advantage of growing up in the pre-Amtrak era and observed the creation of Amtrak for contrast.

Fred was able to meet and then later get close on a personal level with many of the influential leaders who were instrumental in not only saving the industry as we know it today but then reinvigorating it. For instance, his chapter about the late Jim McClellan ("The World According to McClellan") is on point. McClellan was one of the true visionaries that helped create Conrail and then returned for round two by engineering the subsequent break-up of Conrail, which became parts of Norfolk Southern and CSX respectively. Fred was masterful at distilling from a speech McClellan delivered the pungent conclusions that the speaker reached about the realities of railroading in the twenty-first century.

As a journalist with a natural inquisitiveness, Frailey is quick to pose good and often hard questions in an effort to get below the surface and ask why. This skill takes us places other writers cannot. For example, Fred's interview with Rob Krebs ("Watch Rob Run") is remarkable for its insight into why the proposed Burlington Northern Santa Fe–Canadian National (BNSF-CN) merger died stillborn, how Krebs was able to meld two entrenched senior managements from two organizations with vastly different philosophies into one with his merger of Santa Fe and Burlington Northern, and how events in Krebs's personal life affected his own management style.

There were countless articles and columns written by many financial writers and others about the BNSF merger, its integration, and then the failed BNSF-CN merger (which would have been a stroke of genius had the merger gone through). No other writer had the sheer force of will or the ability to delve through the merger's many complexities to get to the heart of the matter. Fred used his natural inquisitiveness to take us behind the scenes to understand why certain decisions were made. He gets us behind the person in the blue suit to understand what makes the individual tick. What other writer could have encouraged Rob Krebs to speak so candidly about his son, Duncan? It also was a measure of the man himself, Krebs, who was so open and genuine with Fred. Fred has a way of having that effect on people who know and trust him.

Likewise, Fred's chapter on Mike Haverty ("Mike Haverty's Long Shadow") is a glimpse into the man who many consider to be a genius by not only having big ideas that bring new revenue into the railroad sphere but by implementing them. As Fred so candidly points out in this piece, Mike was among the last of the breed of class 1 CEOs to come from the operating ranks. (Mike began his career as a brakeman.) The industry is in desperate need of the next Mike Haverty and Rob Krebs.

More than just analyzing railroads and their operations, Fred also enjoys riding trains. His philosophy of having no concerns about how late his train may be is a testament to his unbridled enthusiasm for just being able to live in the moment.

I met Fred at a small reception in Chicago of senior railroad officials more than a decade ago, and I found him to be one of those rare, larger-than-life figures. We got into a conversation about railroads and other worldly matters, and that conversation has been going on ever since. As a youth, I grew up greatly admiring and being influenced by the writing of David P. Morgan, who stood alone among writers of the day and who made *Trains* magazine "The Magazine of Railroading." Today's readers of *Trains* have Fred Frailey as that lens into the railroad industry and reflect what he sees and so carefully observes.

All of us are fortunate that Fred decided to follow in his dad's footsteps to become a journalist and not a railroader. Oh, Fred would have been good at anything he might have tried, including being a railroader. Who knows, he might have been the original E. Hunter Harrison with new and innovative train operations before the world heard of E. H. H. Had Fred gone that route, though, it would have been our loss. The railroad world is richer and wiser for having Fred Frailey out there giving us the candid, behind-the-scenes look into what makes our industry tick—and the personalities behind it. Thank you, Fred.

Thomas G. Hoback
Zionsville, Indiana, November 2018

INTRODUCTION

THAT YOU ARE READING THESE words suggests something to me about both of us: we have an affection for trains and for railroading that transcends childhood infatuations. A lot of kids (my grandson, for instance) develop a fascination for trains at about age 3. I was one of those kids too. The first seven years of my life were spent in a railroad town in southern Kansas, Arkansas City, where trains were an element of just about everyone's life. In a year or two this fascination usually fades away as other interests intrude into our young lives. That describes me as well because my family relocated 350 miles away. Usually that's about it. We go on to other stuff. Does this sound familiar?

But then something happened to me. Now I'm age 10, and I'm riding my bike along the sidewalk of Gilmer Street in Sulphur Springs, Texas. I round a turn and in front of me is a big, black diesel locomotive crossing Gilmer. Its engineer is leaning out the locomotive's window, watching the signals of a brakeman as a coupling is made with freight cars. I stop and watch. Horns honk, bells ring. Back and forth the train moves as the freight cars are sorted. Honestly, it awakened all those memories of my earlier days in Ark City—the big Lionel trainset in our basement, visits to the depot to see Santa Fe's *Texas Chief*, being hoisted onto locomotives by my dad and imagining what it would be like to not get off but instead to leave town.

This chance encounter on a summer day in 1954 became a life-changing event. You can just about draw a straight line from that moment to the book you hold in your hands today. Out of the attic came those Lionel trains, to occupy every usable inch of my bedroom until I graduated from high school. I began to meet the local freights of the Kansas City Southern and Cotton Belt railways. Once the crews knew me, I was invited to ride the cabooses and then the locomotives. By age 12 I collected employee timetables, studied books of rules, and listened on the dispatcher phones as train orders were dictated to station agents. I began to stoke a lifelong interest in the intricacies of how railroads are actually operated. I drove my family crazy.

And it never stopped. As a sophomore in high school I'd declare a mental-health day every six weeks and skip school, driving around East Texas and watching trains. (This lasted until I invited my classmate Seba to join me and we were discovered.) Later, at the University of Kansas, I spent weekends exploring the railroad geography of nearby Kansas City and cultivating the friendships of the men working the region's junction towers. Upon graduation, I took aim at Chicago as a place to live, one obvious reason being that Chicago is the white-hot epicenter of America's railroad world.

In this journey, which continues to this day in my 76th year, I've had a constant companion, the pages of *Trains* magazine. It was my School of Railroading, my secular bible, my key to opening the secrets of what really goes on in this fascinating business. Two men writing for *Trains* sparked my admiration. One was Wallace W. Abbey, a fellow KU journalism graduate of a generation earlier. Wally was a staff writer, traveling the country to write feature stories about whatever piqued his curiosity. In August 1954, 18 pages on the Santa Fe Railway! The following February, 24 pages of everything you'd ever want to know about the Western Maryland! Wally wrote about riding Santa Fe's *Chief* and the Katy's St. Louis-to-Texas fast freight, named the Katy Komet. From my perspective, work for Wally was really having fun.

The job of putting out the monthly magazine fell to Wally's boss, the introverted son of a Lutheran minister. Editor David P. Morgan was a thinker and a poet. On the one hand, his editorial commentaries cut to the quick about issues of the day, whether it be shortsightedness of railroad managements or the sinking fortunes of privately owned passenger trains. On most matters David spoke as an optimist, but he didn't mind writing critically about anyone in a position of power, and railroaders respected him for that. The other side of David Morgan tugged at my emotions. He could put into words what the rest of us felt, be it the mournful cry of a steam locomotive's whistle in the night, the pleasures of a long-distance rail journey, or the finality at the sight of a railroad being taken apart and abandoned.

It's hard for me to express how much, from an early age, I wanted to be a part of *Trains*. My father was a newspaperman, and I happily followed him into journalism. As with any line of work, becoming an accomplished reporter and writer is, for most people, a long process; I did not jump from the womb as an accomplished writer. At times the learning curve became almost painful. I began writing about railroads at the *Chicago Sun-Times*, which hired me right out of KU. The editor of *Midwest*, the Sunday magazine of that newspaper, was always hungry for feature stories and took to accepting my ideas. I wrote about one man's quest to preserve and operate his own giant steam locomotive, about the South Shore Line electric interurban railroad between Chicago and South Bend, Indiana, about Penn Central's new *Metroliners* between New York City and Washington, about the magical upbringing of Santa Fe president John Reed, and about Santa Fe's 40-hour freight train connecting Chicago with Los Angeles. That last story, so amateurishly put together, remains painful for me to reread today. But I was learning. My goal was simply this: to become good enough to write for *Trains*.

At a certain point, I couldn't contain my ambition and decided to make a run for it. This was the summer of 1978. I figured I had one chance to impress Morgan and be asked back to write for him again. Good advice for any young writer is to tackle what you know best, and what I knew best was my home town railroad, known as Kansas City Southern Lines. KCS had been in physical decline for years, and in the early 1970s began to shake apart from neglect. But at just about the time that it might have tipped over and gone down the bankruptcy path alongside the Rock Island Lines and Milwaukee Road, its top management . . . well, I'm getting ahead of my story. Let's just say I had a compelling tale to tell about Kansas City Southern if David Morgan gave me the go-ahead and if the railroad's executives would talk.

He did, and they would. So in October of 1978 I took two weeks' leave from *U.S. News & World Report* and had the time of my life. For three days I got to know the people who ran Kansas City Southern from its namesake city. I also pored over months of daily reports to compile a blueprint of its past and current operating history. Then by train and hi-rail vehicle, I saw almost all the railroad firsthand.

Six weeks later, I mailed Morgan a 10,000-word manuscript. I passed the test, and David spread the piece over the August and September 1979 issues of *Trains*. It was the start of an association with that magazine that lasts to this day. Forget everything else I've done professionally. For me, *Trains* was The Big Time.

Last Train to Texas is a sampling of my hundreds of feature stories, opinion columns, and online blogs for *Trains*. In selecting these pieces, I leaned toward choosing the briefer, livelier pieces over the longer (and sometimes more turgid) stories. I favored stories that entertain. If I detected a flash of humor, so much the better. I want you, dear reader, to have a good time and reach the last page wanting more.

This body of work owes much to the editors who I've worked for at *Trains*. Their support and patience made it possible. Thank you to David P. Morgan, J. David Ingles, Kevin Keefe, Mark Hemphill, and Jim Wrinn. Thank you as well to two articles editors who have found my factual errors, corrected my jumbled syntax, and helped me focus my work, Matthew Van Hattem and Angela Pusztai-Pasternak. Truly, magazine journalism is a team sport. A thank you to the hundreds if not thousands of railroaders high and low who befriended me and thereby shaped the content of my stories. You'll meet many of them in these pages. And of course, thanks to my family, my wife Cathie above all, for putting up with my obsession.

Let's go back to that first two-part story for *Trains*. When I reread it today, I am deflated. Forgive me; it was too long. I put on paper everything I knew about Kansas City Southern and paid too little attention to what the real story was. The real story is how one guy came in and plucked a railroad out of the toilet. I've learned about writing that size doesn't matter. In other words, you can probably tell the same story better in 3,000 words than in 5,000. First, decide what the story is. Then tell it but leave out the dross. That's what I didn't do that first time at bat for *Trains*. In part 1 of this book, you'll find not that first article exactly as I wrote it for *Trains*, but a portion of it, the part I wish I had written decades earlier. It's short enough you won't fall asleep in the telling.

Now come along with me and enjoy the trip.

St. Simons Island, Ga., November 2018

LAST
TRAIN
to
TEXAS

PART I

RUNNING THE RAILROADS

I WOULDN'T MIND RUNNING A railroad. Probably most of us think we could do it better than those who occupy the bosses' offices. A recurrent theme of my columns in *Trains* is to criticize the tendency of railroad management teams to give up investments that would make long-term gains in exchange for the short-term gratification of shareholders in the form of share buybacks and dividend increases.

But to be fair, I've come across many railroad managers and executives I admire, and it is these people you will primarily get to know in the pages that follow. First, there's President Carter—Tom, that is. I've known this man now for 40 years. Retired for about three decades, he remains what he always was, an accomplished yet modest fellow. It was he who wrote back to me in 1978, saying, sure, come visit our railroad and write about it. From that came "President Carter to the Rescue." With that, I became a writer for *Trains*.

Dave Fink ("The Man You Never Want to Cross") is an entirely different railroad executive, one who wasn't afraid to go 15 rounds with his enemies. As he saw it, that's what you had to do to run a railroad in the hostile environment of New England, where traffic pickings are slim and people bear grudges. Given that, I was taken aback by his son David Fink's account of the father's early days at the helm of the Maine Central, when he exhibited both patience and a sense of humor. Do I admire Dave Fink? Probably not. But I've come to respect what he accomplished in building what is now named Pan Am Railways.

Two railroad CEOs I greatly admire are Robert Krebs ("Watch Rob Run") and Tom Hoback ("Thinking outside the Container").

1

I first encountered Krebs when he was chief executive of the Santa Fe Railway and I was writing *Southern Pacific's Blue Streak Merchandise* (Kalmbach Books). Before Santa Fe, Rob's earlier career at Southern Pacific was entangled with this notoriously difficult-to-run transcontinental freight train. Rob spoke of his experiences with the *Blue Streak Merchandise* with such candor that I was taken aback. I mentioned this to him, and I'll never forget his reply: "If I tell you one thing and my employees another, they'll wonder which Rob Krebs to believe." We meet Krebs in the last days of his third railroad presidency, that of Burlington Northern Santa Fe, trying to make one united company from the warring factions of several previous railroads.

Hoback took a woebegone branch line that Illinois Central Gulf wanted to abandon—it's offshoot to Indianapolis from eastern Illinois—named it the Indiana Rail Road and turned it into one of the most successful regional railroads of all time. The story I tell of how his little railroad came to institute a profitable intermodal (ship-rail-truck) operation tells you the way Tom thinks and highlights his stubbornness in pursuit of goals and refusal to ever give up.

Like Tom Hoback, Jim McClellan became one of my closest and most cherished friends. Raised in Texas, he led a life that contradicts what I've been told since my teenage years, that you cannot be a railfan and succeed as a railroad executive. Jim was present at the birth of Amtrak in 1971, helped create Conrail five years later from the carcasses of seven bankrupt northeastern railroads, and a dozen years after that captained Norfolk Southern's breakup of Conrail. A razor-sharp intellect coupled with his gentle but biting sense of humor propelled this man through all sorts of adventures. In "The World According to McClellan," both attributes are on full display.

In these pages, you'll meet Pisser Bill, peer inside the mind of a beleaguered railroad chief executive, and gain insights into managing large (Union Pacific) and not so large (Kansas City Southern) railroads. But I save until almost the end of this section my favorite tale: "When Lou Menk Saved a Zephyr." Menk, who ran four big railroads in his day, was famously against passenger trains. Late in life, when retired, he said to me, "You couldn't make money then, can't make money now, and won't make money ever on intercity passenger trains. That's all there is to it." In other words, Lou thought passenger trains were a cancer whose losses were eating railroads alive. Yet in 1965 he went to bat for the Chicago-Oakland *California Zephyr*, which his Burlington Route ran in partnership with two other railroads. That he would act in contradiction to his strongly held beliefs is a mystery of corporate life we'll just have to accept as probably unsolvable.

Now let us begin at the very beginning of those 40 years with *Trains*.

ONE

—⚏—

PRESIDENT CARTER TO THE RESCUE

ON AUGUST 1, 1973, THOMAS S. Carter became the 12th president of Kansas City Southern Lines (KCS). But few envied him, and why should they? KCS by then was a railroad in name only. Its people could even point their fingers at the time and date that the consequences of years of neglect of the physical plant had begun to visibly bring it down: 4 o'clock on the morning of December 4, 1972. The first winter storm howled over the Ozarks as the brakes of Extra 626 South—three SD40 locomotives, 100 cars, three more SD40s, and 52 more cars—went into emergency crossing Bridge A-206 in tiny Sulphur Springs, Arkansas.

Wind and rain striking his face, the conductor took a lantern and inspected his train. The third locomotive was on the ground. Three cars lay in Butler Creek. Seventeen others straddled the right-of-way north of the bridge. Then an ice storm began. No train would traverse the Second Subdivision for 86 hours.

Later that same morning, No. 77, the first train to attempt to detour around the wreck, turned over its caboose and two cars while backing through the Frisco interchange at Neosho, Missouri. The Pittsburg wrecker, heading toward Sulphur Springs, paused in Neosho to clear up that mishap and derailed itself lifting the first car. On December 7, after taking 93 cars from a siding, a southbound extra derailed eight miles north of Sulphur Springs. Three days later, within sight of that wreck, No. 77 spilled 4 of its 155 cars. Before daybreak the next morning, 3 of the 174 cars of No. 41 left the track at McElhany, Missouri. Back came the Pittsburg wrecker.

All this occurred in eight days on a 34-mile portion of one subdivision, the second. But within weeks, the rash of messy, morale-sapping derailments began to spread. From West Wye Tower in Kansas City to West Yard in New Orleans, from Goodwill, Arkansas, to Greenville, Texas, the rails, the ties, and the roadbed were humped, worn out, rotted, washed away, and mud encased.

Put aside why this came to pass. It's enough to say that railroads then—almost everywhere—were at their low ebb. Their leaders, including William N. Deramus III, president of the railroad and of KCS Industries, its holding company, had just about given up on the business, preferring to take the money railroads generated to diversify into other ventures, sometimes with great success. And in the case of Deramus, he couldn't even see his own railroad, blinded as he was then by cataracts. Bill Deramus knew he needed help.

Tom Carter, a Texan, was a railroader almost from the time he began to shave. He worked for the Missouri-Kansas-Texas—the Katy—part-time while pursuing an engineering degree at Southern Methodist University and before being drafted in World War II. Postwar, post-SMU, he joined the Katy full-time. By 1954, at age 33, he was the railroad's chief engineer. It turned out to be good training for the job that would follow at Kansas City Southern. Like KCS in 1972, the Katy in the mid-1950s was falling apart, in its case largely due to a half decade of drought in its service area that starved it of revenue.

At the start of 1957, Katy's directors, at their wits' end, turned for leadership to none other than William N. Deramus III. Deramus had made a name for himself nursing the Chicago Great Western (a marginal Midwest railroad if ever there was one) back to decent health through rigorous cost cutting and train consolidation. Carter hit it off with Deramus, decades later crediting the older man with saving the Katy from bankruptcy. In 1961, Deramus left the Katy to replace his dad as head of Kansas City Southern. That same year Carter became Katy's VP of operations, broadening his experience. When Carter and a later Katy president, John W. Barriger III, developed irreconcilable differences in 1966, Deramus hired him, eventually to run an equipment-leasing subsidiary at KCS Industries. He was there when, like the Katy, Kansas City Southern fell apart. While staying on as president of KCS Industries, Deramus named Carter as his successor at the railroad. Carter set about doing what good civil engineers do well: devising a plan. And it was expensive—$75 million over three years, in 1974 dollars. That wasn't enough to gold-plate the property but at least enough to lift it out of the muck. The project was capped at $75 million because that was the most the railroad could even dream of affording and strung over just three years because KCS faced an implacable deadline. In November 1976, the railroad would begin running unit coal trains from Wyoming's Powder River basin to three electric-generating stations down its spine south of Kansas City. The revenue would be the railroad's salvation but only if Carter could strengthen the infrastructure in time to withstand the heavy axle loads these trains brought. One pass by a 14,000-ton coal train over the Shreveport-to-Dallas Texas Subdivision then would have destroyed the track structure.

On the face of things, his task seemed hopeless. There was no big bankroll to spend. And Kansas City Southern continued to unravel, January 1974 being the absolute pits. Forty-one mainline derailments occurred that month. More than 200 trains had to be recrewed. By month's end, Deramus Yard in Shreveport, Louisiana, was crammed with 1,576 cars (including 943 loads) waiting to be moved.

Priority number one: patch up the most critical spots. On the Texas Subdivision, for instance, rails were humped in the middle and depressed at the joints, the effect being a roller coaster every 39 feet. Carter had the joints raised and tamped, a violation of standard engineering practice, which says to raise the entire track structure. But there was neither time nor money for such niceties. The roller coasters flatted out a bit, and trains stood a better chance of staying on the rails until a more thorough job could be done.

All those derailments worried Carter. He went to every one. What was going on? Yes, the track was bad, "but we ran into problems that couldn't be explained away so easily." He was looking for a pattern. A disproportionate number of derailments involved midtrain locomotives controlled by the engineer at the front of the train. The accidents tended to occur on the spiral of curves—that is, in the transition from straight track to maximum curvature. They seemed to involve unstable, high-center-of-gravity covered hopper cars. They tended to happen when locomotives (front and midtrain) were working at full throttle.

One night in January 1974, trying to return to Kansas City from a north-end derailment, Carter missed the last plane from Fort Smith, Arkansas. He drove to Tulsa, Oklahoma, and missed the last plane there, too. He checked into a motel, "broke, hungry, sick, and mad." He took a pencil and sheets of paper and began sketching that month's accidents. What was he missing?

"Then it hit me. Of course! The derailments were coming three and four cars ahead of the slave [midtrain] units. That was all I needed. I had the missing link." Carter picked up the motel phone and called the dispatching office in Shreveport. "Stop every slave train at the next terminal and reposition the slaves," he said, reading off a new formula to an incredulous subordinate.

The railroad had been running two-and-two (sometimes three-and-three) combinations of masters and slaves, placing the remote units two-thirds of the way back in trains to equalize air-brake response. This meant that slave locomotives not only pulled the rear one-third of trains up the grades but pushed hard against the cars ahead, too. When track was in better shape, there had been few ill effects. But now slaves were literally pushing unstable cars off unstable track on unstable curves.

The solution to this riddle later seemed so simple that Carter was embarrassed it took him so long to think of it. A few weeks later, owing to an engine failure and a mix-up, a southbound train went up McElhany Hill south of Neosho with slaves positioned in the old manner. Yes, it derailed. From then on, slaves were given more pulling to do than master locomotives, to keep them from pushing, and the precise formula was printed in the next employee timetable, a document all train crew members carried with them.

It probably didn't seem so at the time, but Kansas City Southern passed its low point that January. The derailments that had been bleeding it to death began to ebb, and cash came in faster than it went out. Carter bought new $150,000 tamping machines, instituted better training, and sometimes appointed new supervisors. Armed with trainloads of supplies, a beefed-up maintenance-of-way workforce began altering the face of the railroad. The gangs didn't just place new ties and ballast on the main tracks—they did the passing tracks, too, and then tackled house tracks and industry spurs that hadn't been touched in decades. Not even government-funded Conrail, when it came along three years later, could equal in proportion what Kansas City Southern accomplished after 1973. Ties were replaced at the rate of almost 6 percent a year, double the normal rate. Fifty miles of rail, most of it welded, went into place annually, and the railroad set its sights on one hundred miles. The equivalent of 70 6,500-ton trainloads of ballast was unloaded each year. Centralized traffic control was extended north from Gentry, Arkansas, and south from DeQueen, to cover the entire railroad north of Shreveport.

Slag from Lone Star Steel (on the Texas Subdivision) no longer could be bought in large quantities, and besides, KCS couldn't afford it. So Carter, remembering the high-grade chat that Katy had used, went to Joplin to negotiate an almost unlimited supply for $1.70 a ton. Likewise, he learned that an eastern railroad wanted to sell thousands of tons of 127-pound rail on its right-of-way. Carter bought it at salvage price and had it taken up and shipped to the KCS rail-welding plant near Shreveport.

To the tie-creosoting companies located on or near Kansas City Southern, Tom Carter must have seemed like Daddy Warbucks as he snapped up everything in sight and asked if there were more ties he could buy. Slowly at first, then more rapidly, the results of these efforts became visible, and the pile of temporary slow orders began to shrink.

The work never faltered, not even when the worst post–World War II recession took hold in late 1974. KCS Industries loaned the railroad about $5 million, deferred repayment of additional money the railroad owed it, and arranged a $5 million line of credit with banks. Also, to bankroll the rebuilding effort, railroad dividends had been suspended in 1973; the holding company, which depended upon those dividends to satisfy its own shareholders, kept them happy by distributing oil-drilling stock it owned in lieu of cash dividends.

Still, by October 1975, the recession had bitten deep. Some payrolls were met only by getting quick payment from shippers, and it looked as if the rebuilding would have to stop after all.

To make ends meet, Deramus wanted expenses cut by $250,000 a month. Jerry Gregg, the railroad's general manager, slashed $308,000 a month, primarily by cutting back switch-engine calls and personnel at some locations. At the same time, the railroad went to its employees and asked for suggestions. The response was enormous, says Carter. "A floor sweeper suggested buying a floor-scrubbing machine. We did that and were able to reassign two janitors to more productive jobs." Another employee developed a means to cut fuel consumption by permitting engineers to isolate unneeded locomotives from the main throttle on level terrain or downgrades.

Still another idea was to assign a squad of clerks to recheck waybill computations and rate divisions—a task that had been abandoned in an economy binge years earlier. To its amazement, KCS discovered errors in its favor amounting to more than $200,000 a month.

Such moves as these, together with a traffic rebound at the close of 1975, turned a threatened loss by the railroad into a profit of $1.3 million for that year and got Kansas City Southern over its last financial mountain. His $75 million rebuilding budget well spent, Carter kept pouring money into the property, however. With cash generated by the railroad's improved business levels and more efficient operations (remember, derailments cost big bucks), Carter had invested $165 million in the physical plant by the middle of 1978, according to *Forbes*.

Thus did what *Forbes* called "The Little Railroad That Went Astray" find its way home. As promised, those Wyoming coal trains came calling at the close of 1976, and Kansas City Southern was ready for them. By the end of 1978, roughly 12 loaded trains a week, or almost two a day, headed south from Kansas City, bound for electric-generating plants near Amsterdam, Missouri; Gentry, Arkansas; and Pittsburg, Texas. More coal-hauling contracts at still other electricity plants were in the offing.

Jimmy Carter is rightly celebrated for championing the economic deregulation of railroads. But please give credit to the *other* President Carter—Tom, that is—for the rescue of Kansas City Southern.

August and September, 1979 Trains

TWO

THE MAN YOU NEVER
WANTED TO CROSS

STORIES OF DAVE FINK IN the days when he ran the former Boston & Maine (B&M) and Maine Central (MC) for the majority owner, Tim Mellon, could fill a book, and probably should. Let's just say the man was direct, in your face, and unafraid of a fight— you punch him, expect to be flattened in the counterattack. A bit like Donald Trump, maybe, and Dave made a lot of enemies. I've always thought you had to have a certain amount of those characteristics to survive in running a big New England railroad. New England is a beautiful region but was hostile territory for railroad owners a generation ago.

All this said, I'm always on the prowl for new Dave Fink stories, and I thank his son David for supplying a couple of fresh tales. David succeeded his father and is president of Pan Am Railways, the successor to B&M and MC, and he spoke to a meeting of the North East Association of Rail Shippers a few months back.

Let's go back to 1981. Dave Fink and Mellon have just bought Maine Central, to which they will soon add the B&M (and later the Delaware & Hudson, briefly). Young David is a college student (Northeastern University) with an interest in railroading. So the elder Fink and Mellon ask David to join them in Mellon's battered 1977 VW Rabbit for a tour of the MC facilities in South Portland. They

Pan Am's Dave Fink: In your face, yes, but sometimes with a sense of humor.
Fred W. Frailey

arrive at Rigby Yard's engine terminal. I'll let David continue the story:

I can vividly remember getting out of the car. My father walks over to the engine house, and the first thing he sees is a gentleman tuning up his motorcycle. It did not have a Maine Central pine tree logo on it, so we immediately figured it was not a company motorcycle; it was his personal motorcycle. My father goes over there and asks him questions, befriends him. He didn't know who my father and Tim were.

Person number two was sound asleep with a newspaper over his head, just sleeping. It was a locomotive maintainer.

The third guy we thought was working on a Maine Central project. I remember it was a steel Farm Boss 041 chainsaw. We had the same model, so Dave [the father] goes over and asks him how it was going. Maybe it was brush cutting for signal maintaining. "No, no, it's Friday. I'm getting my chainsaw ready for the weekend. I've gotta get my firewood in for the winter."

You can infer from this that big changes lay ahead for Rigby's engine terminal. I believe it soon ceased to exist.

David Fink also spoke about the old Maine Central headquarters building in Portland:

Beautiful building, but very impractical—no air conditioning and high maintenance costs. My father was never able to see all the people who worked for the railroad. When we came up here, there were maybe a thousand people who worked on that railroad. He called the Portland Fire Department and said we're going to have a fire drill, unload the building so we can do a head count and know who we have. . . . There were a couple of rumored clerks still on the payroll in their late '80s. He wanted to be sure they were still coming into the office.

Those are the stories that are kind of urban lore. And they are true.

And now, my Dave Fink story. In the course of reporting "Pan Am's Second Takeoff" for *Trains* in late summer 2009, I showed up at their headquarters in North Billerica, Massachusetts, for a final chat with the younger Fink. "Want to meet my dad?" David asked. "You bet,"

I said. Off we drove across the state line to somewhere in southern New Hampshire, where Pan Am had a corporate office, and there I met the fellow I once jokingly referred to as "the Meanest Man in Railroading."

I suspect David had been talking to his dad about my visit to the railroad and the conversations we had, and the old man was curious. At any rate, here's this squat, broad-faced, loud-voiced man who, instead of screaming and yelling as mean people are supposed to do, proceeds for an hour to enthrall me with stories of his life decades earlier on the Pennsylvania Railroad (the "Pennsy") and Penn Central. They are stories of screw-ups, misunderstandings, god-awful messes, and unlikely disasters. What all of them had in common were funny endings, and every time Dave got to his punch line, he'd convulse in laughter, barely able to chortle out the zingers.

Utterly disarmed by this encounter, I enjoyed myself hugely. Here's what I wrote about that meeting in my feature story:

> Dave and David, father and son, are a study in contrasts. Dave is an extrovert, David something of an introvert. Dave never seemed to care who he infuriated, David is a diplomat. Case in point: Dave fought Amtrak for a decade over the terms of passenger service between Boston and Portland, Me., whereas David hands out Amtrak t-shirts and wants service extended to Brunswick [which it later was]. But when it comes to running a railroad, they seem to think as one. In hours of conversations, not once did father or son take exception to anything the other said or has done.

Dave Fink, whatever people think of him, is a man shaped by his experiences. At the Pennsy during its decline and Penn Central before its fall, you had to be tough to survive, and that applies even more if you want to run a railroad in New England profitably. Tough would describe Dave Fink well. Mean, no—unless he thought you had screwed him.

May 2018 Trains

THREE

—ᨓ—

WATCH ROB RUN

ROB KREBS SITS IN THE lobby of Washington's Madison Hotel, waiting for a visitor. Open on his lap is a bound (and heavily annotated) copy of the merger application between his Burlington Northern Santa Fe and Canadian National, which he would like to file with the Surface Transportation Board (STB) but cannot. The announcement of this combination set off such a firestorm of hostility from every other big railroad in North America that the STB took the unprecedented step of declaring a moratorium on railroad mergers. Don't even ask to merge, the STB said. Adding insult to injury, United Parcel Service, BNSF's biggest customer, whose trailers the railroad has delivered on time for months without a single flub, had a last-minute change of heart and thinks the deal stinks. Many of his top lieutenants don't like this combination, either, because it threatens the tight-knit culture that Krebs so carefully instilled among the formerly warring "green" (Burlington Northern) and "blue" (Atchison, Topeka & Santa Fe) factions at headquarters in Fort Worth. At times like this, you really know who your friends are. Today, the chairman of Burlington Northern Santa Fe doesn't seem to have many.

So Robert Duncan Krebs is reduced to rereading and refining the merger document week after anxious week while his attorneys seek to have the moratorium declared illegal by a federal court. Imagine his frustration. This is to be the capstone of his career—an end-to-end combination of the two best-run and best-capitalized railroads, in which Canadian National's Illinois Central would fit BNSF's eastern rim like a girdle, extending Krebs's railroad into the heart of Michigan's car-building economy and on to the Atlantic Ocean. By the time CSX, Norfolk Southern, and Union Pacific (UP) fix their own bungled mergers and nurse their balance sheets back to health, BNSF-CN can be a fact of life—and ready to proceed with The Final Merger from a position of strength.

It was not to be, of course. Soon after that steamy summer day in Washington, the appeals court ruled decisively in favor of the moratorium. BNSF and CN called off their merger. "Many people faulted us for the timing," Krebs said later, "and they were right. On the other hand, the stars were lined up, and we gave it a whirl."

And at the end of 2000, the 58-year-old Krebs planned to cede the chairmanship of Burlington Northern Santa Fe to his young protégé, 41-year-old Matt Rose. "I promised my family I would retire by age 60," said Krebs. "I want 2001 to be Matt's baby."

But before you bid good-bye to this blunt, plainspoken man, think for a moment: If you were to be employed by a railroad, invest in one, or ship over one in the twenty-first century, just what sort of person would you want leading that enterprise? Well, you'd want someone with vision, who can see beyond today and imagine a different and better tomorrow. You'd want someone who has felt the crunch of cinders beneath his feet and recognizes BS when he hears it. You'd want someone who has been tested by adversity and grown both as a man and a leader. You'd want someone who has his story straight and tells everyone the same thing. In other words, you'd want someone at least a bit like Rob Krebs.

His thunderbolt temper hasn't made Krebs easy for everyone to like. Nor does the fact that he's smarter than most people he encounters (and doesn't conceal that fact) endear him to a lot of folks. But give this man a break. Again and again the past dozen years, Krebs confronted business challenges that would wilt most executives. Every time, he has emerged with his integrity intact and the railroad he led stronger. And for good measure, along the way he has become a better man.

In June 1997, 80 BNSF senior executives gathered on the campus of Texas Christian University (TCU) in Fort Worth for the strangest meeting in that young railroad's 21-month history. Several months earlier,

Krebs had initiated a series of sessions for these people and their spouses at Colorado's Aspen Institute, a Rocky Mountain think tank whose programs are designed "to enhance the participants' ability to think clearly about the complex issues they face in their society and organization, mindful of the primacy of the moral perspective." In what for railroaders could only be described as a bizarre experience, they read the works of Western civilization's most provocative thinkers—the likes of Locke, Plato, Aristotle, Hobbs, Keyes, Martin Luther, Martin Luther King Jr.— and then in seminars related this wealth of ideas to BNSF. What does liberty mean to BNSF? How does equality square with the way we run this railroad? What are our moral duties to our coworkers?

This is not railroading as your father knew it, but from those sessions emerged BNSF's vision statement, defining what the railroad's customers, employees, shareholders, and communities should expect from it. Krebs carries this statement with him always and believes every word of it.

Krebs was driven to this project by two recent events in his life. One of them crystallized at a meeting he held in 1996 with employees in Havre, Montana, an important terminal on the former BN. "I brought them great news," he recalls.

BNSF is now here. You are part of the most wonderful new company that is going to grow. We are going to take this stepchild, the High Line route, and add capacity. We are going to station more locomotives at Havre, and business will grow, and your lot in life will improve. Then I open it up to questions, and it dawns on me there are a bunch of people in this room still pissed off that Great Northern and Northern Pacific had merged in 1970. They aren't even on the same page as me. I'm trying to sell a merger, and I'm one merger behind. This was symbolic. Frankly, there were definitely differences in the senior management group, too.

How many companies born of mergers have had their vitality sapped by us-versus-them conflict? Think back to the Red Team and Green Team when the Pennsylvania Railroad combined with New York Central in 1968 and how it turned out. Such rivalries have haunted every rail merger since, and the green and blue factions were at war in at HQ Fort Worth, too. Former BN people felt like conquered vassals. As one ex-BN executive puts it: "We bought them, but they took us over." To BN folks, the Santa Fe way of doing things was "ready, fire, aim." Santa Fe people felt that Burlington Northern executives studied problems to death . . . and then some. There was, in other words, much mutual disrespect. Krebs knew he had to stem the infighting and get everyone to pull together. "What we had to do," he later said, "was establish a community. A community has shared values. We had to agree on what they are." The TCU meetings, lasting a day and a half and moderated by John P. Kotter, a professor of organizational behavior at Harvard University's Graduate School of Business, were to give shape to the philosophical issues discussed in Aspen. Three big questions about running the company remained unresolved: Should BNSF be centralized or decentralized? What business should the railroad emphasize—grain and coal or intermodal? And should its leader be (in his words) Darth Vader or Mary Poppins?

Krebs could never have undertaken these meetings—would never have even considered talking about such squishy subjects as liberty and equality and duties to employees and communities—but for another event that hit really close to home. Duncan Krebs, the youngest of his three children and the apple of his eye, was having trouble growing up. Duncan needed special schooling to help him mature emotionally, and that led the Krebs family to the Hyde School, in Maine. Hyde School teaches personal responsibility and character development. Hyde also demands participation by parents, in let-it-all-hang-out group sessions.

"This was very difficult for me," says Krebs, not used to unburdening his feelings or his family's dirty laundry in front of strangers. "The first time they went around the circle of parents and kids and got to my wife and me, we were asked, 'What are the issues in your family?' I said we didn't have any issues—we're perfect people." He wanted to mean it, too.

That's where Rob Krebs started. "Several years later, I'm a changed man, a different person than I was even at Santa Fe. Hyde School changed my life." At the most superficial level, he cooled his famous stack; now when he loses it, the victim gets an apology. (Hyde changed his son's life, too. Duncan Krebs is now a senior at Bucknell College in Pennsylvania.)

At those Hyde School sessions, Krebs grew as a person by learning to speak honestly and to hold nothing back. Maybe the same honesty could unite his railroad's fractious management. Those two days at Texas Christian, the BNSF people let it all hang out. "Why are we in the intermodal business? It slinks," one person would say, and the arguments would ensue. As hours passed, raw emotions emerged. People lost their reticence and began speaking their minds in front of Krebs. Instead of snapping back, he listened. "Most of the pent-up outbursts came from former BN people, who felt they were on the outside looking in," says a participant. Says another:

> It got down to somebody telling Rob, "You think this or that." And Rob said, "You don't know what I think. For instance, I have never said what I think of the former BN culture. But I will tell you what I think." And he told everybody what he thought of [the former BN chairman Gerald] Grinstein—that he was a decent fellow who didn't have a clue about how the railroad was run, that he was tending to the higher corporate elements and making sure the trappings of the job were always available to him, and that BN couldn't have lasted much longer with that kind of leadership. Turns out a lot of BN people thought the same thing.

(Krebs will not comment on what was said by anyone at TCU.)

The BN side argued for the coal and grain business; the Santa Fe side, for intermodal. The BN side wanted Krebs to be a warm Mary Poppins; the Santa Fe people had become accustomed to his Darth Vader toughness. Opinions were all over the lot regarding centralization. Finally, the moderator, Kotter, summed things up: "First, will you be centralized or decentralized? The answer is both. Should you go after unit-train stuff or intermodal? Yes. Should Krebs be Mary Poppins or Darth Vader? Yes. Now"—and here he got to his real goal—"I want all of you to raise your right hands and repeat after me: I hereby swear that from now on I owe my allegiance to Burlington Northern Santa Fe, and I will never again utter the B-word or the S-word, because that's BS."

With that, the meetings ended—and so, claims Krebs, did the infighting. Others who were there largely agree. "He kept forcing our vision, our direction, our style," reports a vice president. "He didn't want two styles of railroading around here. And he knew that unless you talked about the values you'd adopt and settle on them and publish them, they'd be meaningless." Or as another executive puts it more bluntly: "Before, we had a management team that just didn't get it. We didn't even like each other very much."

The proof they could work together as a team came soon enough. Just weeks later, transportation-management software was cut in to finally let the company run its two railroads as one. At the same time, Union Pacific's own merger with Southern Pacific blew its operations apart, sending a flood of UP customers to BNSF. Though it bulged and shuddered from the onslaught of new business, BNSF never fell apart. You must give some credit for this to the team-building efforts of the boss.

Rob Krebs will leave BNSF defeated in one respect, which returns us to the Madison Hotel and that merger application in his lap. This he believes: without a national reach, no railroad will ever realize its full potential, and the industry will remain an unattractive alternative to most shippers. Short of that ideal, no railroad will hold its own destiny in its hands.

Krebs was incredulous when he read the STB's proposed new rules on mergers. BNSF and CN could have cleared those hurdles easily. And look, he adds, now the bureaucrats want to drag out the process to consume close to two years. "That's untenable," he says. "I can understand tough criteria, but give us a break on the delays." In this environment, why bust the bank adding capacity when you can't earn a decent return on that money? BNSF is using every loose dollar to buy its own stock—a better investment in the face of these uncertainties, Krebs says, than shiny new rails.

So it appears Rob Krebs has met a force he cannot control. The national network he believes in so fervently is viewed with abject fear by his customers and with icy indifference by the regulators. Maybe it's time to get out of the way and let somebody else try. Step right up, Matt Rose. But love Rob Krebs or hate him, someday you're going to miss this man.

January 2001 Trains

THINKING OUTSIDE THE CONTAINER

IN THE THIN AIR OF a late afternoon in early December, you're aboard an Indiana Rail Road train, heading toward Indianapolis. As the engineer Brent Sexton rounds a sharp curve, you peer back from the lead SD90 and watch double-stack containers roll into view—52 in all. You're entitled to ask: What on earth are they doing on a small regional railroad?

In his 29 years as a railroad entrepreneur, Tom Hoback pulled off his share of near miracles. In 1986, he bought from Illinois Central Gulf (ICG) its Indianapolis branch, a dilapidated, almost impassible appendage that ICG had tried to abandon, and turned it into the fabulously successful Indiana Rail Road. Then in 2006 his railroad bought and began breathing new life into Canadian Pacific's Indiana line, a coal-hauling route built by the Chicago, Milwaukee, St. Paul and Pacific Railroad (the Milwaukee Road) a century earlier. That deal got his railroad into Chicago by trackage rights. Today, any Class 1 railroad would love to boast of Indiana Rail Road's low operating ratio.

But for sheer audacity, it's hard to top his latest thing. Hoback figured out how the Indiana Rail Road can become profitable in the intermodal business on a 155-mile haul. This is no easy feat. Intermodal is a low-margin business. There's not a lot of revenue to cover costs. Moreover, in a maximum of four hours, these containers could have been trucked to Indianapolis from Chicago, which is what used to happen.

The longer the haul and the greater the number of boxes double stacked on your train, the better the odds of making a profit. At least

Indiana Rail Road's intermodal trains swap engineers in Switz City, Indiana, in December 2014. This service succeeds because its speed from Chicago to Indiana is not the issue. *Fred W. Frailey*

that's the conventional wisdom, as is the truism that intermodal is a game for Class 1 railroads only. So this is the story of how, after 20-plus years of plotting, imagining, negotiating, and going back to try again, this little railroad upended conventional wisdom.

Some of those containers behind you on train HWSA began their journey toward Indianapolis 24 days earlier, on November 8, 2014, aboard the China Ocean Shipping Company (COSCO) container ship *Cosco Philippines*, from the port of Qingdao, China. Others were added when the ship departed Shanghai two days later. On November 21, the ship made its first North American call at Prince Rupert, British Columbia.

Eight-year-old Prince Rupert Container Terminal is important to this tale for three reasons. First, it is the closest port in North America to Shanghai—68 hours sailing time closer, in fact, than Los Angeles. Second, it is served exclusively by Canadian National Railway. And third, it was not Hoback's first, second, or even third choice as a way to break into intermodal.

In 1990, Southern Pacific (SP) approached him to ask if the Indiana Rail Road would participate in a Los Angeles–Indianapolis routing, using Illinois Central (IC) as an intermediate carrier between East St. Louis and Newton, Illinois. Hoback was excited, but a package of pricing and service eluded the three railroads. (In 1996 SP became part of Union Pacific, and in 1999 IC was bought by CN.)

Hoback didn't let go of that thought. What if SP interchanged Indiana-bound containers with Canadian Pacific Railway (CP) in Kansas City, Missouri? Hoback approached CP, which was interested enough to offer the use of a Piggy-Packer tractor at the smaller railroad's Senate Avenue Terminal in Indianapolis. But the routing from Kansas City to the crossing of the Indiana Rail Road in Linton, Indiana, via Chicago, was slow and circuitous, and obvious questions about reliability arose. "Again," says Hoback, "we just weren't able to make the economics or service work."

You're probably wondering: Why even bother? CSX Transportation runs directly from East St. Louis to Indianapolis, and there's an intermodal terminal at Avon Yard on the west edge of Indiana's capital city. Why hadn't it locked up this business from the West Coast?

The short answer is that CSX (and before it, Conrail) wasn't interested. In fact, Indianapolis has never been much on the minds of Conrail and CSX intermodal people. The Avon ramp is in the middle of the yard, where it interferes with rail operations. A bigger impediment to running containers into Indianapolis from Asia might be called the Class 1 mind-set. East St. Louis to Indianapolis, at 237 miles, is small potatoes to a railroad like CSX and hardly worth the bother. Eric Powell, Indiana Rail Road's manager of intermodal and economic development, knows of only one shipper that gets containers from Asia to Indianapolis in this manner, and this retailer must arrange a dray of its containers between the UP and CSX ramps in East St. Louis. CSX prefers the longer hauls to and from Indianapolis from the Northeast.

Hoback got another taste of Class 1 thinking when he approached BNSF about building an Indianapolis block of containers on double-stack trains out of Los Angeles and adjacent Long Beach, for interchange at Clearing Yard in Chicago. The bigger railroad's first reaction was one Hoback would hear often in his search for a partnership: Oh, we already serve Indianapolis, through our Chicago terminals. BNSF wasn't interested.

But there was another problem, explains Pete Rickerhauser, a retired BNSF vice president for network development who was advising Hoback. "BNSF is all about high-density lanes connecting high-density throughput terminals, turning freight as fast as possible," says Rickerhauser. "Anything that detracts from that model—offline destination, not daily, not real high volume—they think detracts from the core model."

One attribute of Tom Hoback you probably now sense is that he doesn't easily give up. The Indiana Rail Road reaches Clearing Yard through trackage rights over CSX from Terre Haute, Indiana, which it inherited when it bought CP's Indiana Line. He toyed with starting ramp-to-ramp service between Chicago and Indianapolis. A host of obstacles stood in the way. Indiana Rail Road's trackage rights extend to Clearing and only Clearing, and the owner, Belt Railway of Chicago, has no intermodal ramp. Plus, few shippers want intermodal service just between Chicago and Indianapolis, cities that are closely connected by interstate highway. Add to that service inconsistencies on this route and the pile of added costs, and there went that idea.

Early on November 25, four days after arrival, the containers leave Prince Rupert as part of Canadian National train Q198. Destination: Chicago. A delay of this length is unusual, Powell says, and is caused by diversions of container traffic away from even more congested US ports. "We've had boxes stay in Rupert as few as 26 hours," he says. A day earlier, other containers delivered to Roberts Bank, British Columbia, near Vancouver, by Maersk and Hapag-Lloyd shipping lines, left for Chicago on train Q116.

Both trains reached Harvey Intermodal Terminal in Chicago on November 29, the Saturday after Thanksgiving. The boxes were reworked into a single Indianapolis block of cars and moved Sunday morning to adjacent Markham Yard, where they were coupled to other freight cars headed for the Indiana Rail Road.

A bit after noon that day, CN train M371, which originates in Flat Rock, Michigan, near Detroit, stopped to pick up the Indianapolis-bound cars and spotted the block in Effingham, Illinois, 175 miles south, that evening. As it happened, no local CN crew worked at Effingham that night, so train L531 didn't cover the final 21 miles to the Indiana Rail Road on the Newton branch until early Tuesday morning. In Newton, at 2:55 a.m. on December 2, Indiana Rail Road train PAUT2, a turnaround job from Palestine, Illinois, took possession. Tom Hoback's container train was now on home rails.

Today these handoffs occur almost effortlessly. But it took years to reach this point. Canadian National is one of Indiana Rail Road's major connections, at Newton, and Hoback makes regular visits to CN headquarters in Montreal to nurture that relationship. "I was struck by how proud they were about their quality of service from Prince Rupert," he says. Furthermore, Hoback learned that 80 percent of the containers coming into Rupert were destined not for Canada but the central United States. Hold it! he thought. That's us—Indiana. But when Hoback first broached the idea of an all-rail routing from the Pacific Ocean to Indianapolis, he got the usual Class 1 blowoff: "Oh, you know, we serve Indianapolis from Chicago. Customers love it, and it's only . . ."

Hoback knew the customers didn't love getting their boxes in Chicago, because he had been talking to them for years and could recite their dissatisfactions. Average transit time from Shanghai to Indianapolis via California was 27 days and sometimes far longer. The boxes that came via Southern California would get stuck there—or lost there. Same thing at the big new intermodal terminals next door to each other southwest of Joliet, Illinois: BNSF's Logistics Park Chicago and UP's Global IV, both small cities unto themselves. Says Hoback: "Containers would get caught in those terminals, and customers would have to pay extra to truckers to make emergency runs to central Indiana. They were having terrible times getting consistent deliveries."

So when the CN people gave him the cold shoulder, Hoback came right back to them with a list of 80 companies in central Indiana interested in all-rail service. "It turned out," he says, "CN was only moving containers to one customer of the 80 we identified."

That was the eye-opening turning point. "To their credit," says Hoback, "the more we explored intermodal service to Indianapolis, the more interested CN's people became. We were a much bigger market than they thought. We also told CN that they are really constrained where their intermodal market can grow because they don't have a big footprint. We enlarge their footprint. Within a two-hour dray of downtown Indianapolis, you can reach Cincinnati and Louisville and Dayton."

More than two years elapsed before the first intermodal train reached Senate Avenue Terminal in July 2013. The two railroads had to agree on a service plan that could be executed without hiccups and agree on a division of revenue. At its end, Canadian National worked with steamship lines to institute seamless Asia-to-Indianapolis service offerings. And at the other end, Hoback's people had to line up a customer base and persuade them to alter their shipping arrangements, to use Prince Rupert (and later Vancouver, CN's other Pacific port).

PAUT2 (that's Palestine Utility 2, better known as "Paulie 2") covers the 29 miles from Newton to Palestine in 90 minutes, arriving at 4:25 a.m. Its crew stows the train, the back half of it those 52 double-stack containers, on a side track before heading home. At 5:55 a.m., Bob

Cooper, the conductor of PAUT3, enters the Palestine yard office, followed a few minutes later by the engineer Dan Ayers. Cooper assembles the paperwork and studies the switch lists for 30 minutes; then Ayers boards the lead SD40-2, and they begin drilling the yard. Three hours later, they've reassembled the train, added two GP38-2 locomotives to the two SD40-2s, and departed Palestine. At Glenn, Indiana, 24 miles east of Palestine, their train juts northward onto the Midland Subdivision for 8 miles before reaching Hiawatha Yard in Jasonville, Indiana, on the former CP line (CP called this locale Latta).

At Hiawatha, the train is again switched and assumes its final identity, HWSA. Engineer Sexton gets his train moving at 4:20 p.m., retracing the path taken by Paulie 3 over the Midland Sub a few hours earlier. Now the containers are on the front of the train, inasmuch as it reversed direction at Hiawatha. HWSA swings back onto the Newton-Indianapolis line at Glenn and heads northeast toward Indy.

But not for long. At Switz City, Indiana, 11 miles farther along its route, its opposite number, SAHW, awaits at the east end of the siding. Sexton and the engineer Frank Rodriguez, who brought SAHW from Indianapolis, trade trains. Sexton will bring the SAHW to Palestine, where tonight's PAUT2 crew, coming on duty at 8:00 p.m., will take the double stacks and other cars to Newton for interchange with CN.

At 8:55 p.m., HWSA stops a mile from Senate Avenue, and Rodriguez ties down his train. A switch crew coming on duty at 11:00 will spot the double stacks along two 1,400-foot pad tracks. Containers will be ready for pickup at 6:30 a.m. the next morning.

So what's the takeaway? First, the genius of this whole idea is not to focus on the transit time from Chicago to Indianapolis (two days, which is tortoise speed) but on the transit time from Asia to Indianapolis and a seamless ride for customers' containers, which avoid offloading in Chicago and go right to downtown Indianapolis, without a lot of angst and missed arrival times.

Second, Indiana Rail Road makes this work through extraordinary cost control. Those containers ride on preexisting trains running on preexisting schedules. Added operating expense: zero. The only cost becomes that of Senate Avenue's ramp, and that cost diminishes in importance as volume grows. Hoback won't say what his railroad gets per container, but he does say that the operating ratio (OR) of the intermodal service is 80 percent, which means operating costs cover only 80 percent of operating revenues, making the operation quite cash positive. Moreover, that ratio is falling as volume goes up. (The railroad's overall OR is impressive, 61 percent, Hoback adds.)

A big contributor to that profitability is the surprising volume of backhaul business to Asia. An empty container going to Shanghai is a cost to be borne—the fate of roughly 85 percent of containers that Western railroads handle from Asia—whereas a filled box is more revenue to offset costs. "When we announced the service," Hoback says, "agriculture companies called to say they wanted to ship animal feed, soya, back to Asia, where there is huge demand." Another popular product is dried distillers' grains, a byproduct of making ethanol that is also in great demand in Asia as a supplement to animal diets. Also being backhauled: hardwood veneers, delicate to handle in open cars but deemed safer inside containers. Relatively few containers go home empty from Indianapolis.

Tom Hoback retired in June 2015, selling to CSX that part of Indiana Rail Road that it didn't already own. In his almost 50 years in the railroad business, Hoback did many amazing things. But nothing demonstrates his tenacity better than this tale of how he made a success of intermodal transportation on his little railroad, in the face of almost total indifference by larger connecting railroads.

May 2015 Trains

FIVE

THE WORLD ACCORDING
TO McCLELLAN

I ENJOY JIM McCLELLAN'S SPEECHES. Hell, I enjoy Jim McClellan's company. First of all, he has a finely developed sense of humor, which he likes to turn on himself. More important, Jim has a talent for distilling huge numbers of facts and ideas into simple truisms. Finally, like Zelig, he had a talent for appearing at so many critical junctures of railroad history the past half century. He was present at the development of what became Santa Fe's *Super C*, the fastest freight train ever. He was present at the creation of Amtrak and later of Conrail. He was the brains behind Norfolk Southern's brilliant (and savage) attack on the purchase of Conrail by CSX, an attack that succeeded in getting Norfolk Southern (NS) more than half of Conrail.

Jim has been retired from NS for about a decade, where he ended up as VP of corporate strategy, but that mind of his keeps churning. And it was on full display at this week's annual meeting of the Lexington Group, in Peoria, Illinois. Rather than give you a traditional report on his talk, I'll just offer you some sound bites. Ladies and gentlemen, the world according to Jim McClellan:

"A simpler network runs most efficiently."

"You make money by running big trains and keeping them in motion."

"When railroaders talk merger, they don't pull out their financial statements. They pull out their maps."

"Railroads used not to think of themselves as profit-making enterprises. They thought in terms of public service. Santa Fe and Seaboard Coast Line stuck with passenger trains way beyond the time they knew they shouldn't be in that business, because they thought it their duty."

"The goal of regulation [in the Interstate Commerce Commission era] was fairness, not efficiency. It was a convoluted, complex, and inefficient system. There were too many routes, too many railroads, too many junctions. In the end, the system was unsustainable."

"Penn Central: two drowning men clinging to each other."

"Two railroads are all you need for competition. This idea once seemed radical."

"The most important event in railroading in the Midwest during the 1970s was the liquidation of the Rock Island Lines. It sent shockwaves through labor. Ten thousand jobs went poof."

"And Canadian Pacific acquired the Delaware & Hudson. God knows why they bothered."

"Unit trains concentrated traffic on a few main lines, as did intermodal traffic."

"Marketing guys now have to deal with what it *really* costs to run a railroad."

"The decline in coal traffic is good for railroads. It will force them to find new markets. Railroads don't like to do that, because they don't have enough intelligent sales people."

"There are a million ways to make railroads more efficient. But none of them are easy. It will require lots of singles rather than home runs."

"Transload and intermodal give customers a whole lot of alternatives to poor carload service."

"Transcontinental mergers? I think not. The threat of reregulation is serious. And the economics of such mergers are not compelling. We're down to about ten junction points between major railroads, and they run well. The railroad network today is pretty efficient rather than Balkanized."

"Railroads thrive on density and velocity."

That's it, folks. Wish you could have been there. But for those who were not, you now have the best of McClellan.

(My friend Jim McClellan died on October 14, 2016.)

October 5, 2012 TrainsMag.com

THE SAGA OF "PISSER BILL"

SURELY ONE OF THE STRANGEST collisions of my lifetime occurred not between trains but between personalities. On one side was
William F. Thompson, vice president of operations of the St. Louis–San
Francisco and then of Burlington Northern upon their 1980 merger.
Even his enemies conceded that the Texas native was close to brilliant,
able to achieve more production out of maintenance-of-way gangs and
mechanical shops than anyone else of his era. His most important
student became a young Frisco assistant trainmaster named Hunter
Harrison, who went on to run four Class 1 railroads. Harrison always
credited Thompson with teaching him Railway Economics 101.

But the respect that Thompson got on the Frisco (and before that,
on the Terminal Railroad Association of St. Louis and Rock Island
Lines) he never received on Burlington Northern. Hence the other
side of this collision: the officials who ran BN before Thompson got
there. They were polite, collegial men, by and large, who might argue
among themselves but with mutual respect. They were proud of their
accomplishments in the decade after BN's creation, particularly
developing the Powder River basin coal franchise, a gamble with
$2 billion of borrowed money. They despised Thompson, seeing him
as a cigarette-smoking, whiskey-belching, foul-mouthed, disrespect-
ful tyrant—in the words of one BN guy, "a throwback to the despotic
regimes we had learned about in our studies of world history." But
also, perhaps, a somewhat typical railroad-operating man from the
South, where you had to be loud and abrasive to get your way.

In this culture clash of epic size, not only did the BN train and engine service guys hate Bill Thompson, so did their bosses and their bosses' bosses. One division superintendent in that era called him "over-the-top crude."

There was method to Thompson's vulgarity. "How else can I get peoples' attention?" he once said. "And if you think I'm mean now," he added, "you should have seen me at the Frisco; they needed shaking up, too."

So did BN, by all accounts. The new president of BN's holding company, Richard Bressler, came from the oil industry and was unimpressed by BN's operating results. BN had spent prodigiously to expand its capacity to run heavy coal trains, and all that Bressler saw as a result was one of the highest operating ratios in the West. Where are the shareholders' yachts? he might have asked. Bressler expressly wanted Thompson and Thompson's boss at the Frisco, President Richard Grayson, to run the merged railroad. And I suspect he wanted them to kick butt and achieve results. They did both in short order. In four years, Grayson and Thompson chopped the bloated head count from about 49,000 to 40,000 and drove the operating ratio from a high 92.1 to a respectable 78.7.

But at what cost? The incident that earned Thompson his nickname, one that he never shook, occurred at the roundhouse in Spokane, Washington. Or was it in Mandan, North Dakota, or Teague, Texas? I've heard numerous places named as the locale. Thompson gets worked up at something he doesn't like, turns to his retinue of officials, says, "Here's what I think of this place," and, unzipping the fly of his dark suit, proceeds to urinate into the turntable pit.

Word of the unprecedented act sped through BN. With equal speed over the Compass computer system came a bit of doggerel penned by a person unknown but later said to be a train dispatcher in Missoula, Montana. Titled "Ode to a Jerk," here are excerpts:

> I remember well the night he came, and it became his claim to fame.
> A group of men did follow him, and bow they did, to every whim.
> Into the roundhouse they did go, and just in time to see a show.
> He belched and cursed and yelled and farted, but that stalwart group, they never parted.

*He yelled some more and threw a fit, unzipped his fly, and pissed in
the pit.*
"Close down this place," he did proclaim, never faltering in his aim.
The news, it traveled very quick; it made some laugh, it made some sick.
*I know this doesn't sound quite right, but I kid you not, it's the truth
all right.*
His name thus earned, he bears it still, and now is known as Pisser Bill.

And so we end this tale of woe; into that pit I will not go.
I've worked in grease, I've worked in dirt;
I've worked when well, I've worked when hurt.
I'll work in pits, where snakes do hiss;
but I won't work in old Bill's piss.

A BN vice president who reported to Thompson read "Ode to a Jerk"
and feared he would be ordered to remove it from every crew-room
bulletin board in his region. Sure enough, Thompson called him. "They
wrote a poem about me," he said. "Did you see it?" Yes, replied the vice
president. "Well," he said, "now they know who I am." And Thompson
just laughed.

June 2014 Trains

Union Pacific's Jim Young: From "what's in it for me," to "what's in it for us."
Fred W. Frailey

—ₘ—

A MAN IN FULL

JIM YOUNG, THE RETIRED CHAIRMAN and former chief executive of Union Pacific, died at 61 of pancreatic cancer. It's a vicious disease that is rarely detected before it spreads to other organs; then it is incurable. Through good care and stout heart, Jim was lucky (if you can call it that) to live almost two years after his diagnosis. He had given up the CEO job immediately after learning of his illness and retired as chairman of the board nine days before his death.

Raised in Omaha and educated at the University of Nebraska, Young knew only one employer as an adult, so far as I can determine. Joining UP in 1978, he worked his way steadily up the ladder of vice presidencies, becoming chief financial officer in 1999, president in 2004, CEO in 2005, and chairman in 2007. Here was a class act. "He was the best boss I ever had," says Mike Hemmer, the retired vice president of law. "I feel honored to have worked for UP during his era of integrity, openness, and vision."

Young was elevated to the presidency after a dark chapter in the company's history. In 2003, UP hired few if any new train and engine employees and continued not to hire them in its Western Region into mid-2004. Then the railroad seized up in a combination of a business boom and severe crew shortage, initially in the Western Region and then systemwide. The lost revenue and added expenses came to hundreds of millions of dollars. In 2003 UP hit an earnings-per-share benchmark that triggered the forgiveness of millions of dollars of loans to the railroad's top officers. Was this a coincidence? You tell me.

That wasn't the way Jim Young governed. I've heard him described any number of ways. Allow me to synthesize what I've heard and observed: Before Jim Young, Union Pacific was a great company but less than it could be. It was everybody for himself. What Young did was try to bend the culture of Union Pacific, from "what's in it for me" to "what's in it for us." To quote Hemmer: "He inspired all of us to believe we could be transformationally excellent yet remain genuine. UP was one of the best places in America to work from 2005 to 2012 because of the tone he set at the top." Frankly, I've never seen a chief executive described in such a, yes, loving manner. But what Mike says is totally consistent with everything else I know about the man.

I interviewed Jim several times by phone, but in person only once. We sat, barely two feet across from one another, in UP's Washington office. I don't remember the questions I asked in that interview or his answers. What I will never forget is the translucence of the skin on his face and the intensity of his pale blue eyes; they drilled right into me. I cannot imagine anyone talking one-on-one with Jim Young and not being truthful.

But did he succeed in bending the culture? Certainly for the short term. We'll only know many years from now whether the change was forever.

February 16, 2014 TrainsMag.com

EIGHT

MIKE HAVERTY'S LONG SHADOW

KANSAS CITY SOUTHERN ANNOUNCED IN the summer of 2010 that Mike Haverty, 66, had relinquished the post of chief executive officer to David Starling, who had been president and chief operating officer. Starling would run the company, but Haverty would remain in the new position of executive chairman, which struck me as a transitional role leading to his retirement in 2015.

The succession at KCS marked a significant turn for the railroad industry in North America. Since the dawn of railroading, at least one sizable company (and sometimes most of them) was run by someone coming straight from operations to the corner office. Mike Haverty was almost the last of that breed among the Class 1 railroads (Norfolk Southern's Wick Moorman started in engineering). So permit me to say a few things about this man.

Haverty would never have been voted Mr. Congeniality by his fellow railroad CEOs. He was tenacious and unrelenting in pursuit of his railroad's goals. Nor was Haverty always easy to work for. "I'm a demanding boss," he has said. Still, I've always admired the man, in part for his creative business abilities but also for his infatuation with the history and traditions of this crazy business. It was Mike Haverty who put warbonnet paint back on the faces of Santa Fe Railway locomotives in 1989 while he was that railroad's president. He reintroduced the late-1940s freight locomotive colors to KCS almost two decades later. And he assembled at Kansas City Southern a business car train that is the handsomest of them all; the Deramus family that ran this railroad for three generations would call it their own.

But it's his business acumen that impresses me most. I'll cite three examples, starting with J. B. Hunt Transport, today BNSF Railway's biggest customer. Haverty once told me how that relationship began at the Santa Fe:

> I had gone to visit Hunt in Lowell, Arkansas, a couple of weeks before he was scheduled to attend a meeting in Chicago. In Lowell we convinced him to have his team stop by our Santa Fe headquarters for a visit and then take a trip on an intermodal train between Chicago and Kansas City the next day with one of his trailers riding on a car just ahead of the business cars.
>
> We had locomotives painted in the revived warbonnet scheme all shined up and on the head of the train. It wasn't long after we left Corwith Yard that we were flying at high speed while Interstate 55 was congested with traffic. We observed how smoothly the J. B. Hunt trailer was riding ahead of the business cars.
>
> When we passed through Galesburg, Illinois, we shook hands and said we had a deal. We got up to $30 million in revenues before the lawyers finalized the written contract.

Putting aside United Parcel Service, this joint venture became the biggest partnership between a big trucker and a railroad. BNSF's Matt Rose should call Haverty once a month to thank him for that missionary work.

Just months after Haverty became president and CEO of Kansas City Southern in 1995, KCS bought a 49 percent interest in the 154-mile Texas Mexican Railway, operating between Laredo and Corpus Christi, Texas. KCS didn't come within hundreds of miles of the Tex-Mex. What was Haverty thinking? He soon made it very clear: Kansas City Southern wanted to span both the United States and Mexico.

For this to happen, Haverty had to hit back-to-back home runs. One would be to connect KCS to the Tex-Mex—that is, gain ownership or trackage rights between Beaumont, Texas, and Corpus Christi, as a condition to Union Pacific's purchase of Southern Pacific. Then he would have to win a bidding war against the far larger UP for Mexico's

2,400-mile "northeast concession," running south from Laredo and Brownsville, Texas, to Mexico City and the Pacific Ocean. Few people—me least of all—thought he could succeed.

Lo and behold, when the Surface Transportation Board approved the SP-UP combo, it attached almost no strings that UP had not already agreed to, except to give trackage rights from Beaumont to Corpus to KCS-owned Tex-Mex. This got KCS to the Mexican border.

Then late in 1996, KCS and its Mexican partner, Grupo TMM, outbid UP by (according to Haverty) a margin of almost three to one for the 50-year Mexican franchise (renewable for another 50 years). Everyone said KCS had overpaid. Haverty replied that time would tell, but said, "It wasn't exactly luck." Years of confusion and acrimony with Grupo TMM followed; KCS eventually bought out its partner. Only after almost a decade and a half did KCS de Mexico start to become what Haverty envisioned. Ultimately, I think the $1.4 billion paid for this franchise will be judged an enormous bargain.

And finally, there's the Meridian Speedway, the east-west line between Meridian, Mississippi, and Shreveport, Louisiana, that KCS acquired in 1994 from MidSouth. Trouble was, KCS lacked the money to make this potentially superior route for southeast-southwest traffic what it needed to be. Then Haverty had an idea, which he calls a "franchise access fee." As he put it to me years ago: "If you're going to get access to that corridor and extend your franchise, you're going to have to pay for that right—a capital fee." Norfolk Southern was then seeking a way to extend its reach on intermodal business to Dallas. So Haverty brought up the idea to Wick Moorman, the new NS CEO, and thus was born the Meridian Speedway LLC, an intermodal-automotive partnership, of which NS owns 30 percent and invested $300 million.

A lot of railroad chief executives have come and gone without ever having ideas of this magnitude. Haverty not only had those ideas but executed them, with far fewer resources at his disposal than the other Class 1 freight haulers.

October 2010 Trains

HOW TO GO BOOTS UP IN
RAILROADING

JIM JUSTICE, YOU NEED TO meet Randy Parten and Ed Ellis. Parten
is a Texas oil man who, in the late 1980s, assembled 50 passenger cars
for luxury trains to move vacationers from the Denver airport to the
resort town of Aspen, Colorado. Parten made one mistake fatal to his
cause, however: he committed his capital and talked up his idea before
getting the support of the Denver & Rio Grande Western Railway,
which owned the tracks. No such support came through. So much for
his Roaring Fork Railroad.

In more recent times, Ed Ellis, the founder of the Iowa Pacific
Holdings group of shortline railroads, believed he was coming to the
rescue of Denver skiers when he agreed in 2009 to assemble cars and
locomotives to replace the Denver–Winter Park, Colorado, Ski Train,
whose equipment the owner, Philip Anschutz, had sold to Canadian
National. Ellis, too, committed his money (and sold tickets) before he
had a signed contract with Amtrak to provide a crew, insurance, and
indemnity for the operation. Days before inauguration, Ellis was humiliated when Amtrak, rightly or wrongly, pulled the rug from under
him. Ed at least had the satisfaction of winning $1.1 million in damages
from Amtrak in a civil suit tried before a jury in federal district court.

Do you see a pattern here?

Now comes Jim Justice, owner of the Greenbrier Resort, a failing
business he rescued after CSX, the West Virginia hotel's former owner,
put it into bankruptcy in 2009. Justice, who made fortunes in farming

and coal mining, is possibly the richest man in West Virginia. He, too, was bitten by the dream of running luxury passenger trains, in this instance between Washington and White Sulphur Springs, West Virginia, initially one day a week in each direction. So bitten, in fact, that he and his partners, Ross E. Rowland Jr. and Paul Nichini, committed $15 million of Justice's money to buying and rebuilding 15 passenger cars once used by the American Orient Express and GrandLuxe Express.

Once again, where's the signed agreement? Nowhere in sight, unfortunately. The three partners, doing business as Greenbrier Express Co., are part of a complete and utter mess involving Amtrak, Buckingham Branch Railroad, CSX, and Norfolk Southern, the latter three being railroads that the *Greenbrier Presidential Express* would traverse.

In a nutshell, here's how matters stand. Greenbrier Express thought it had Amtrak's agreement to operate the train under its existing contracts with the three railroads, as an "extra," albeit one running on a weekly schedule. As part of that agreement, Amtrak would provide insurance and indemnity coverage. But Greenbrier doesn't have a contract, after some 15 months of waiting for one. Besides, not so fast, say Buckingham Branch and CSX. Buckingham Branch wants longer sidings so freight trains won't suffer long delays waiting for the Greenbrier train. CSX believes the Federal Railroad Administration has ordered Greenbrier to negotiate separate terms for the operation of the train with each railroad. Through a spokesman, FRA insists it made no such order and disavows what CSX is saying. Yet Amtrak continues to believe the CSX nonsense about the nonexistent FRA edict. To its credit, NS appears to be observing all this from the sidelines. So do you believe me when I call this a complete and utter mess? Finally, if one is to believe Ross Rowland, CSX isn't interested at all in negotiating terms with Justice for running the once-a-week round trip. It just wants Justice, one of the railroad's biggest shippers, to simply go away.

Today, I got Randy Parten on the phone from Texas. Randy is now many years older and wiser. His fleet of passenger cars is but a memory, except for two cars residing on his ranch. He confirms that he never got to first base with Rio Grande's president at the time, Bill Holtman. "He never would see me. He never answered a letter I wrote. Yet he badmouthed me all over Denver as someone who would never pay his bills." But Parten insists he did not err by buying the cars before getting the railroad on his side. "If you don't spend money up front," he says, "nobody believes you're serious."

Parten has some advice for Jim Justice and his partners: "What you have to do is decide whether your service is really causing a railroad problem or whether a railroad is just throwing red herrings at you. If you are causing real problems, you have to fix them, or nothing will get done. Then you've got to unruffle the feathers and get everyone singing from the same hymn book."

Good words, those. Randy's last remark to me: "I miss the railroad business, but I'm never going back in it."

(In 2016 Jim Justice was elected governor of West Virginia. We're still waiting for the Greenbrier Presidential Express.)

September 28, 2011 TrainsMag.com

TEN

THE BATTLES OF POWDER RIVER

WITH THE CLARITY OF 20/20 hindsight, you can lull yourself into believing that the Powder River basin as a source of railroad coal traffic was always meant to be and that developing this Niagara of new business from Wyoming was easy. The truth is that nothing about Powder River was ever preordained or easy. In an atmosphere of fear, uncertainty, and doubt, a few railroaders who really cared about their businesses made it happen.

History could have taken many other paths. What if Congress hadn't just passed a Clean Air Act that made low-sulfur coal from Powder River attractive? What if Burlington Northern's chief executive, Lou Menk, had lacked the courage to bet his company's future on developing this new business? What if regulators had denied railroads the rates they needed to cover the true costs of hauling coal, which include track maintenance on a scale never imagined? On and on the what-ifs go. How all this came to happen hinged on a few critical junctures.

At the time of Burlington Northern's creation in 1970, coal from a vast subbituminous bed was just starting to be shipped in unit trains out of Wyoming and Montana. But where would the mines be concentrated? Close to Sheridan, Wyoming, and points north? Or near Gillette, Wyoming, and points south? By 1972, the answer became clear, as BN built a 16-mile branch line financed by the minerals firm Amax, from Donkey Creek, Wyoming, just outside Gillette, to a new open-pit mine named Belle Ayr. The branch wasn't built to high standards. Loaded trains returning to the main line had to surmount a 1.25 percent grade, which meant pusher engines. Had BN located the branch five miles to the east, to follow Caballo Creek toward Belle Ayr, a lot of future operating problems would have been avoided. But Amax balked at the cost, and BN gave way, because the enormity of what lay ahead wasn't quite clear. It was as if, blindfolded, BN touched the tail of a Bengal tiger and thought it had found a Persian kitten.

By 1973, the blinders were off. Energy companies competed for mining rights along a line running straight south from Belle Ayr, where 70-foot-thick seams of extremely low-sulfur coal lay close to the surface. They all wanted rail service, PDQ. Getting it to market, however, would be a huge undertaking, and the least of the challenges would be building rails to the new mines. At first, you see, BN thought of the coal from Belle Ayr as incremental business—a train a day. Its line from Lincoln, Nebraska, to Billings, Montana, which passed through Gillette, already hosted three of four general freights a day and was good for one more. But the track structure, laid with 112-pound-per-yard jointed rail atop light-duty roadbed, would be quickly put to waste by the pounding handed out by multiple 10,000-ton coal trains.

It became apparent to BN's people that they needed to rebuild practically all of their main routes or risk seeing the railroad fall apart. There was very little welded rail anywhere on BN, and it had let the pace of tie replacements lapse. At the conclusion of a budget meeting in 1974, Robert Downing, vice chairman under Menk, leaned over to Ivan Ethington, vice president of operations, and said, "The wolf is at the door, and we're not doing enough. We need a plan."

Ethington gave the assignment to the industrial engineer Jerry Pinkepank, and in two weeks, Downing had his plan. It was to spend $2 billion by the end of that decade to extend the Belle Ayr branch 111 miles through the coal fields to join another BN route and provide a second, southern exit for coal and to upgrade the rest of the railroad. Problem was, a severe recession had begun. BN didn't have $2 billion or even a fraction of that sum, and the board of directors was divided over whether it was prudent to spend that much money. After all, Bechtel Corp. was making a full-throated effort to gain the right of eminent domain for its coal slurry pipeline, which might make Menk's railroad irrelevant.

In one of those real-life miracles, everything went right. Menk got his board's approval to build what is now the Orin Subdivision, or Joint Line, and to jump-start the rest of BN's infrastructure. (Two directors who had little faith in the future of railroading quit in protest.) To find the money, BN hired as assistant vice president of finance Raymond Burton, a wizard who convinced the federal government to let railroads sign leveraged leases to finance locomotives and coal cars. Then Burton sold bonds, leveraged leases, trust certificates, and two issues of preferred stock, ultimately financing the whole package (by then $2.3 billion). BN's day was saved, and Ray Burton later became chief executive of Trailer Train (now TTX Co.). Oh yes, coal slurry was a bust, never leaving the starting line.

A postscript: On July 1, 1980, Richard Bressler arrived from ARCO, the energy company, to run Burlington Northern. He knew nothing about railroads, however. On his fourth day at BN, the new CEO came to Gillette to meet the Alliance Division superintendent, Bill Greenwood. The two men hi-railed through the coal fields. Not an hour into the trip, Greenwood recounts, Bressler turned to him in their vehicle and said: "If I had been CEO at the time, we would never have done any of this investment in coal."

BN's Lincoln-to-Billings line skirted the north edge of what is now the Joint Line. Chicago & North Western's (C&NW) line to Casper and Lander, Wyoming, skirted the south edge. There, the similarities end. To reach the coal, near Douglas, Wyoming, C&NW trains had to brave 544 miles of the Nebraska Division, or Cowboy Line, from the juncture with Union Pacific at Fremont, Nebraska. Laid with rail as light as 60 pounds per yard and often lacking ballast, the Cowboy was as decrepit a route as you could imagine. Ed Burkhardt, North Western's assistant VP of transportation in the early 1970s, made an overnight business car trip from Chadron, Nebraska, to Casper about 1973. "It was a slow trip," he says. "The next morning, I asked the division manager how he slept. Not a wink. I told him I slept fine, and he replied, 'You didn't know what we were running over.'"

On a lark, almost, North Western sent the Interstate Commerce Commission (ICC) in 1973 a competing application to build north into the Powder River basin to reach the same mines that BN wanted to serve from the other direction. Litigation could have lasted forever. But this time, the bureaucrats got it right. ICC commissioners called in BN's Downing and North Western president Larry Provo and told them they would approve one application, but not two. The two men were put in a room together to make up their minds. Both of them, rather than risk being shut out, emerged with an agreement to jointly own the Orin Subdivision between Coal Creek Junction (26 miles south of Donkey Creek) and Shawnee Junction on the south. (The limits were later moved 11 miles north to Caballo Junction, for a total joint ownership of 103 miles.)

C&NW was beyond poor, somewhere on the far side of destitute, and would remain so for years to come. To meet payroll, it periodically scrambled its people to round up all the scrap metal they could find. Moreover, it was unfocused. In his memoir, *12,000 Days on the North Western Line*, civil engineer Gene Lewis depicts a railroad that kept forgetting the importance of getting into the coal fields and claiming its share of the revenue gushing forth. Time and again, Lewis recounts, he'd hear from those above him on the totem pole that the Powder River idea was dead. But the corpse kept coming back to life, if only feebly.

North Western's problem was securing financing. It dawned on Lewis, however, that C&NW could build or rebuild 107 miles to reach Union Pacific's North Platte Subdivision and not have to rehab the Cowboy. In June 1976, aware of Lewis's idea (code-named Project Yellow), Provo called UP's president, John Kenefick, and suggested that UP become his railroad's partner and help finance it.

Kenefick was encouraging, but four months later Provo died of lung cancer, and his successor, James Wolfe, offered little direction, Lewis says. When UP and C&NW people met in March 1977, UP proposed that North Western sell its rights to the Powder River basin route to the larger railroad in exchange for a cash settlement and a royalty of 8 cents a ton (about $800 per train), according to Burkhardt, who was present. Talks broke off, and North Western again considered the impossible: upgrading the Cowboy across Nebraska. BN, meanwhile, completed the Orin Subdivision, today's Joint Line, on October 6, 1979.

North Western's Wolfe, however, became crafty like a fox. He had the railroad apply for a $275 million Federal Railroad Administration loan (later upped to half a billion), to rehab the Cowboy and pay off BN to gain entry to the Joint Line. Getting that much money out of the feds was a near impossibility. But the smokescreen Wolfe fanned around his go-it-alone plan—hiring an engineering firm to oversee the Cowboy's reconstruction, ordering materials, and the like—may have helped lure Union Pacific back to the table to discuss Provo's original idea of a joint venture and connector line to Joyce (South Morrill), Nebraska.

The two railroads struck a deal in early 1980. BN cried foul—the deadline North Western had agreed to for paying up had expired—but the ICC ruled that agreement anticompetitive and invalid. With UP's backing, $414 million in private financing was a cinch, and the first North Western train left Antelope Mine on August 15, 1984. Five years late, C&NW had entered the game.

Interviewed in 1972 by *Business Week*, Norfolk & Western (N&W) president John Fishwick remarked that BN was setting its coal rates much too low. He insinuated that BN didn't know much about what we now call heavy-haul railroading. Lou Menk was livid at the public dressing-down. According to the journalist Rush Loving, Menk had BN's car shops fashion a silver-speared trash picker-upper of the sort that people use when cleaning roadways (N&W had launched a high-profile effort to clean its rights-of-way) and sent it to Fishwick. "After all, Jack," Menk's letter concluded, "you never know what might happen if you bend over."

Yet Fishwick was right. When it originally set rates from Powder River mines, BN used a dull pencil, grossly underestimating the spending needed to keep its coal routes to the east and south in working order. By the time it had bought hundreds of locomotives, built new shops, and upgraded thousands of miles of track, it realized the gravity of its miscalculation and ratcheted rates up sharply. Naturally, the electric utilities on the receiving end of these rate increases reacted to the pokes in the eye, and war was on. In a sense, that war is still being fought.

The battle with the city of San Antonio over coal from Cordero Mine to Elmendorf, Texas, lasted a dozen years. San Antonio's rate per ton rose from $10.93 in 1976 to $23.05 in 1980. The city went to the ICC yelling foul against BN and delivering carrier Southern Pacific. Ultimately the railroads refunded $70 million, but not before Congress got involved by legislating special relief for the public utility. (In 1985, San Antonio got revenge, signing with Chicago & North Western.)

The rate paid by Arkansas Power & Light (AP&L, now Entergy) to White Bluff, Arkansas, went from $12.78 per ton in 1979 (AP&L protested that it was too high) to $18.75 in 1981 and $22.62 in 1982 (to a sister plant in Newark, Arkansas). That rate case dragged on at the ICC for years, and before it was over AP&L was also a North Western client.

BN also locked horns with the Omaha Public Power District in 1982 after raising its rate between Rawhide and Caballo mines and Arbor, Nebraska, 53 percent. To adjudicate this, the ICC established a new policy for rate setting in cases involving no competition. Regulators said to *imagine* that a competing railroad existed and to calculate the costs this efficient competitor would incur between the same origin and destination. By then, ironically, there really was competition from North Western and UP, and BN cut its new rate 40 percent to keep Omaha Power's business.

With North Western on the scene, the balance of power over rates shifted. For roughly two decades after 1984, those utilities that could played BN off against North Western (and later BNSF Railway against Union Pacific). As contracts came up for renegotiation, it wasn't whether the utility would get a lower rate from one or another of the railroads but how much lower a rate. Finally, in 2004, Jack Koraleski, UP's executive vice president of marketing and sales, remarked that so little profit was left in the coal business that, given the choice of running a grain train or coal train over his capacity-constrained railroad, he'd choose the grain.

Starting in 2004, as their networks filled up, railroads regained some of their pricing power. They briefly toyed with abandoning long-term contracts and instead publishing public tariffs—here's what we charge between X and Y, take it or leave it. And they ceased to reflexively try to steal each other's business at every opportunity.

Electric utilities, having enjoyed 20 years of pricing power in the Powder River basin and losing it, haven't given up. They are the biggest supporters of railroad reregulation by Congress. And in a sense, the bad blood all dates back to that showdown in San Antonio.

April 2010 Trains

The *California Zephyr* awaits departure in 1967 from Denver on Burlington Route partner Denver & Rio Grande Western. *Steve Patterson*

ELEVEN

WHEN LOU MENK SAVED A ZEPHYR

IN HIS LONG RAILROAD CAREER, Louis Menk ran four big railroads: Frisco, Burlington, Northern Pacific, and the newly created
(in 1970) Burlington Northern. He was unafraid to make momentous
decisions and comfortable with his opinions. One oft-repeated opinion
he voiced to me late in his life was this: "You couldn't make money
then, can't make money now, and won't make money ever on intercity
passenger trains. That's all there is to it."

At the Frisco, Menk sought in the mid-1960s to discontinue its
entire network of passenger trains and succeeded in ridding the company of all but two pairs of trains. Then late in 1965 he became Burlington's president. The Chicago, Burlington & Quincy (CB&Q) had
the most aggressive passenger sales force in the United States, run
by Bill Burke but energized by his assistant general passenger traffic
manager, Herb Wallace. Wallace, a born salesman, was a fountain of
ideas. About the time Menk showed up, Wallace wrote a prospectus
on how to relaunch the anemic *Kansas City Zephyr* between Chicago
and its namesake town; the train was being beaten to death by competition from Santa Fe.

Anyway, Menk immediately splashed cold water on all the Burlington passenger train promotions, such as special trains to take Chicago-
ans to Colorado for the weekend. And to prove his point that passenger
trains lost money even at CB&Q, he hired a consulting company
whose team included W. Edwards Deming, an engineer, statistician,

and management consultant credited with teaching the Japanese after World War II how to manufacture quality products.

Deming labored long and hard to document each and every cost of running passenger trains, down to how many minutes it took to switch the *Nebraska Zephyr* in Galesburg or the Kansas City–Omaha locals in Omaha. In the end, the consulting company reported that Burlington's passenger fleet produced net income of $4.5 million in 1964, the period under study. By the time this was reported in 1966, however, Menk was long gone to Northern Pacific. Likely, he never read the report he commissioned.

I hope I'm not boring you, but I wanted to make the point that Lou Menk did not tolerate passenger trains very well. In clearing out our house in Virginia in 2016, I came across a letter Menk wrote to Myron Christie, his counterpart at Western Pacific (WP). Burlington, Rio Grande, and WP jointly operated, beginning in 1948, the Chicago-Oakland domeliner *California Zephyr*. The train was beloved by one and all. But by 1966 losses on WP by the *Zephyr* were starting to strip Western Pacific, the smallest of the three railroads, of its profits from running freight trains.

I want to reproduce the letter Menk wrote to Christie on April 28, 1966, because in it a man who professed to dislike passenger trains refused to endorse cutting off the foot, so to speak, of his flagship first-class train. Here goes:

> At our meeting in Chicago, April 19, you informed Mr. Aydelott [Gus Aydelott was president of the Denver, Rio Grande & Western] and me that it was the intention of the Western Pacific to file an application for the discontinuance of the operation of the California Zephyr between Salt Lake City and Oakland. Burlington feels that such a course of action is unwise, impractical and untimely for a great many reasons, a few of which I shall attempt to outline herein.
>
> First, however, lest there be some misunderstanding concerning my philosophy in regard to deficit passenger operations, I think I should define my personal feelings in these matters. As you know, I spearheaded what was perhaps the largest passenger-off case heard by the I.C.C. since the 1958 law has been in effect. The results were by and large successful. Therefore, it should be recognized that

I feel very strongly that a railroad should not be obligated to operate substantial deficit-producing passenger service which does not serve the public interest.

I am, however, a realist as well. The case on the Frisco was vastly different than the service now under consideration. In the case of the California Zephyr there is a comparatively high occupancy rate. On the Frisco it was very low. By comparison the losses in connection with the Frisco operations were very high, yours are low, and in fact have declined. The Zephyr serves an area which attracts the traveling public. That was not true in the Frisco case. I could go on and on ad infinitum.

So much for what I personally feel. We here at Burlington feel that already we have made some concessions which by your own record have resulted in a decline in your alleged loss. Our feeling is that not enough time has elapsed for those measures to be fully effective.

While we might or might not question your loss figures, it is almost a certainty that in a proceeding before the Commission the opposition will, with probable effectiveness.

Whether we like it or not it is a certainty that the opposition will relate the improving profit picture of Western Pacific to this case.

Finally, you I know are aware as I am of this administration's feelings on the subject of passenger trains. At a meeting last winter the President himself was quite definite, therefore my feeling with respect to timing.

You might also relate the Southern Pacific experience to what might be your own.

We honestly feel that there is a future for this type operation if we maintain the quality of service and at the same time consider and make economies that appear to be possible.

It is therefore my duty to inform you that Burlington will not support an application for discontinuance of your operation and while we would do so with great regret, we probably would take a formal adversary position in any such proceedings.

With best personal wishes,
Louis W. Menk

By its own accounting, Burlington earned almost $200,000 operating its end of the *California Zephyr* in 1965, although that would turn abruptly to a loss of $283,000 in 1966, the year of the letter. Menk by April 1966 must have sensed that the economic tide was turning against this train.

So why did he write this remarkable letter? I suggest we take him at his word—that the deck of political cards would be stacked against letting this popular train be taken off at that time, so why incur the public wrath? Western Pacific nevertheless went ahead and sought without success to be rid of the *Zephyr*. WP tried again in 1968 and once more hit a wall. Finally, in 1969, it sought a third time to remove the *Zephyr*. Remarkably, even then WP's passenger department still employed 252 people, all devoted solely to this train! In 1969, Western Pacific's losses from operating the train more than consumed the railroad's operating income.

The *California Zephyr* ceased to run west of Salt Lake City early in 1970. Interestingly enough, through all of this, neither Menk or his successors at Burlington ever joined Western Pacific's efforts to discontinue the train and in fact operated it with Rio Grande as a triweekly Chicago–Salt Lake City domeliner right up to the start of Amtrak in May 1971. Without that unwavering support, the *California Zephyr* would have disappeared as a through train years earlier. Thank you, Lou, because I realized my goal of riding the train the entire way mere months before that became impossible.

I hope you have enjoyed this little look inside the machinations of the railroad business half a century ago, this parting of the curtains that lets those of us on the outside peer inside to see the people on the other side who call the shots. It all goes to show that you should judge people not by what they say but by what they do.

May 27, 2016 TrainsMag.com

INSIDE THE MIND OF MICHAEL WARD

SOMETIMES YOU WONDER WHY YOU ever wanted the job. What a fix your company is in. And it's not just about CSX Transportation. You could as easily be Lantz Fritz at Union Pacific or Jim Squires at Norfolk Southern. Or the chief executive of any other US Class 1 railroad. We all direct enterprises that are in a world of hurt. It's 2016, and the bottom has fallen out of our businesses. What in the heck do you do?

You have done all the easy things. You laid up locomotives. (And gosh does it hurt to take delivery on new $3 million machines you ordered ages ago when you have hundreds of others stashed in storage.) You have trimmed capital spending, slashed the crew boards, consolidated divisions, lengthened trains, and raised rates to the point customers are in mutiny.

But for all that, you are still swimming against the tide. Just look at the latest weekly numbers for CSX: coal off 33 percent versus a year ago, petroleum products 41 percent, metallic ores 25 percent, and so on and so on. Even intermodal—your salvation, you keep telling yourself—is off 5 percent the latest week. Look longer term? The year-to-date numbers are even worse, an unbroken string of minuses, commodity by commodity, except for autos, waste, and (barely) intermodal.

When you suggest to your marketing people that they ease up on rate increases and accept new carload business on lower profit margins, your CFO threatens to quit, arguing that rate hikes and higher margins are the only thing you've got going for you. You've hounded the intermodal guys so hard they run at the sight of you, but look what good that does. The truckers are in a slump, too, and with cheap diesel fuel, their rates are as low as yours in some instances. That means you have nothing to offer them that would entice their boxes onto your trains. You envy the western railroads and their long, long hauls.

You put your strategic planners to work on how a Conrail-type combination of your coal franchise with that of Norfolk Southern might work. That is, put the coal businesses of both railroads together and spin them off to shareholders or as a wholly owned subsidiary of the parent companies, to market coal in any direction, not just established routes. But the Coal Department got wind of this and isn't cooperating, insisting the business will come back. You got your start in the Coal Department and think otherwise, but it goes to show how hidebound railroads are—throw out any new idea and you get ten reasons why it won't work and none why it might. Think outside the box? Your people are so terrified they can't even think inside the box.

The other day you got to thinking. CSX is one big jumble of underused assets: cars, locomotives, freight yards, people—you name it. Why not go on a carload sales blitz and bring in anything that covers avoidable costs or better? This is business it won't cost a penny of capital to get because you've got capacity to spare. The operating ratio would go up, due to smaller profit margins, but so would earnings, and isn't the bottom line what this is all about? Send the marketing boys and girls into the field and, prospect by prospect, customer by customer, put those assets of yours back to work. Canadian Pacific just did this—3,000 cold calls in three months.

You're so pumped up by this idea that you're actually smiling when you go down to the marketing floor to lay things on the table. But by the reception you get, you'd have thought you had announced CSX wanted to merge with Canadian Pacific. We can't lower our rates or accept thinner margins, you were told, because that would undercut our existing rates with some of the same customers.

But you fought back with your marketing people. Not just coal, but our whole base of business is shrinking, you argued. We've got to replace what goes away, or we may as well go out of business. And it's your job, you said, to find these customers, even if we have to accept slimmer profit margins. Get out there in the field! I'll cover your backs with investors, you told them.

And do you know what they said? Boss, we don't have anyone in the field. We're all here in Jacksonville. We phone the big accounts, and once or twice a year we tell everyone what the next rate increase will be. That's what we call marketing these days. So, Mr. Ward, your idea of a sales blitz can't happen because nobody knows how to beat the bushes.

You retreat, deflated, to the executive floor and close the door. What other options for reviving your railroad do you have? Well, there's always Hunter Harrison at Canadian Pacific. He sought a few months ago to merge with Norfolk Southern. Why not CSX? For just an instant you think of getting Hunter to the phone. But then you remember: even if you were serious about making a deal with CP, it will never fly. You and Fritz and Squires poisoned the waters about mergers with the politicians, regulators, and customers, to keep Canadian Pacific away from Norfolk Southern. They bought your hype so completely that you've made it impossible for anyone to suggest a merger now.

You wonder about the trap that ensnarls you and your contemporaries at the other railroads. The relentless focus on lowering the operating ratio has everyone slashing costs, raising freight rates on existing business, and setting rates on new carload business that sometimes exceed what truckers charge. How to get out of this trap?

Well, that's for another day. Or for divine inspiration. Again you ask: What to do?

(In February 2017, Michael Ward announced his retirement. Weeks later, Hunter Harrison, formerly of Canadian Pacific, became president and chief executive officer of CSX.)

July 2016 Trains

THIRTEEN

THE LEGACY OF
HUNTER HARRISON

WE WOULD ALL AGREE THAT he was a genius at breaking down railroad operations to its simple components and running trains economically. Hunter Harrison learned railroading at the knee of a brilliant, profane Texan, William "Pisser Bill" Thompson, who was on his way to becoming VP of operations of the Frisco in the late 1960s when Hunter encountered him at Tennessee Yard in Memphis. "Young man," said Thompson, spreading his arm toward a sea of freight cars, "what do you see out there?" "A lot of good business, Mr. Thompson," replied Harrison. Retorted Thompson: "What? Good business? See, that's the difference, Hunter. I see a bunch of delayed cars, and you say it's good business." Hunter Harrison retold that story the rest of his life, which ended unexpectedly in mid-December 2017 of complications from a respiratory disease.

From lessons such as this, Harrison learned inventory control and asset utilization. Later, within Burlington Northern's Seattle Region, he tried before others did at running individual cars strictly by schedule, thereby getting better utilization of equipment, including locomotives. Later still, running operations at Illinois Central, he put into practice all the ideas that had been brewing within him, including balance—if you run a train east, run one west, and better yet, have them meet midway and swap crews, thereby ending away-from-home expenses. He later did his magic at Canadian National and Canadian Pacific and upon his death was eight months into remaking CSX.

So, a genius at railroad operations, yes. But was the man a genius at running a railroad? Running a railroad, after all, is about more than running trains. You have to consider retaining your customers and finding new ones, dealing with government, building high morale, and on and on and on. No, he was not a genius, and in fact I would call the man merely ordinary in some aspects of being a chief executive and deficient in a few critical areas. To say this does not detract one iota from the respect I have always shown for him. We are all imperfect creatures.

Harrison was so focused on operations that other aspects of the CEO's job may simply have bored him or conflicted with his operating policies. His big blind spot at Canadian National was customers, getting them and keeping them. He insisted customers load cars seven days a week. The natural traffic cycle is low volume Sunday and Monday, building to a crescendo on Friday and into Saturday. This played havoc with his desire to achieve operational balance, running the same trains every day, each way, and thereby always having cars, locomotives, and people in the right place.

To force customers to play the game his way, Harrison had his marketing vice president, Jim Foote, institute low rates for early in the week and successively higher rates through Friday. It worked, I guess, but at the cost of alienating the customers, who were bludgeoned into changing their way of doing business. One of the first things Claude Mongeau did upon becoming Harrison's successor in 2010 was to publicly apologize for the way customers had been treated and pledge to turn over a new leaf, which CN did.

Later, at Canadian Pacific, Harrison's blind spot became politics. You may recall he tried to publicly entice Norfolk Southern's new chief executive, Jim Squires, into agreeing to a merger of their railroads. Squires didn't just say no, but hell no, and to make sure Harrison got the point, he put the full weight of Norfolk Southern's formidable Washington, DC, office into poisoning the well within the federal government. The effect NS had in Washington must have stunned Harrison, who told me years earlier that visiting Ottawa or Washington was "a waste of time." CP did not have a Washington office, just a law firm that did lobbying under contract. Harrison, clueless to the intricacies of the political process, was publicly humiliated and gave up his grand plan to get the final round of mergers rolling.

But give the man his due. What Mongeau did at CN was keep Harrison's operating practices intact while instituting more customer-friendly policies, along with some sophisticated initiatives that wed the railroad to the specific logistical needs of customers. The result is the hugely successful Canadian National you see today. Harrison's protégé at CN and CP, Keith Creel, now chief executive of Canadian Pacific, is giving marketing and customer relations the attention that his former boss did not. I expect good results. Hunter Harrison's practices modified by customer-friendly policies are a win-win combination.

This brings us to CSX and 2018. Did Harrison put the railroad on the right path or leave it in shambles, having ripped its practices and institutional knowledge almost to shreds while not living long enough to build a new foundation? I wish the former but suspect the latter.

His former colleague at CN and now his successor at CSX, Jim Foote, has his work cut out for him. I interviewed Foote in 2009 and thought him whip smart and funny (meaning a quick thinker). Nowhere in his background is experience in operations. And operations is where CSX now stands exposed.

Lastly, I wish Hunter Harrison had been better during his Hunter Camps at teaching people how to think like him rather than to act like him. It's an important distinction. In other words, you can tell me what to do (Hunter Camps), but how do I learn to think like you? Maybe that is our biggest loss.

March 2018 Trains

—w—

A BATTLE FOR SUPREMACY IN THE WEST

CSX IS STRUGGLING, DRIVERLESS TRUCKS are on the horizon, and the railroad world seems in disarray. Let's talk about something that works: railroading in the West. Let's talk about BNSF Railway and Union Pacific.

We have here two magnificent companies, each well run and hugely profitable. Their differences are what interest me. Why, for instance, has BNSF's business over time been growing and Union Pacific's shrinking? And why, despite this, does Union Pacific consistently report more operating income than BNSF—shouldn't it be the other way around?

Part of the explanation may lie in something neither railroad controls: route structure. Explains Chip Paquelet of Skylands Capital: "If I were able to invest in both railroads today, I'd buy Union Pacific. Managements change every seven to ten years. Therefore, so can management practices. The one thing that cannot change is who has the best route structure, and it's Union Pacific."

Ownership affects how the railroads are run, too. Publicly held Union Pacific falls captive to the short-term focus of Wall Street. The analysts want to know what will happen the next quarter. The thinking goes: if you have a long-term vision for your company, tell it to your kids because we're not interested. This isn't Union Pacific's fault. BNSF since 2010 has been a wholly owned subsidiary of Berkshire Hathaway, whose chief executive Warren Buffett is famously committed to the long term and largely ignores Wall Street. Every year the railroad writes Berkshire Hathaway a check—the amounts vary between $2.5 and $4 billion—and Executive Chairman Matt Rose sends Buffett a quarterly letter keeping him abreast of what's going on. Otherwise, Rose and Chief Executive Carl Ice are pretty much left to run the railroad as they see fit.

Constantly under Wall Street's gaze, UP's focus is the profitability of its business—the term used is "reinvestibility." In other words, UP asks if the rate it gets on new and even existing business is sufficient to pay for and replace the equipment and other assets used in handling it. If not, UP isn't interested. I don't know what the rate of return is that Union Pacific demands, but let's just pick a number: 18 percent. Union Pacific, in other words, isn't out to be the biggest railroad. It just wants to be the richest. This has been the guiding principle at the company for at least a dozen years.

BNSF also wants to be the richest railroad, obviously. But it seeks to get there by another route, which I call baking a bigger pie. I cannot prove this, but I believe that Rose, Ice & Company read Union Pacific pretty clearly. BNSF's strategy is that if it can bring on new business and increase market share *and* over time increase the profitability of that business, BNSF will grab it, even if the rate of return is less than what UP demands. (BNSF is also not above poaching Union Pacific's portfolio, although of course Rose publicly denies doing so.)

I'll offer an example: coal. Coal for power plants is under pressure from two directions, air-quality regulations and cheap natural gas. Railroads can't do anything about regs. But they do serve power plants, mostly in Texas, that can switch between coal and gas as fuel. Union Pacific's stance has been: here's our rate—take it or leave it. BNSF is willing to do what Rose calls "gas deals." Instead of losing a plant to natural gas, BNSF modifies its contracts so that the rate goes up and down in line with the price of natural gas. This way the railroad keeps the business (and maybe picks up a Union Pacific customer or two) and still makes money.

So those are the two approaches being employed in the West. UP emphasizes profitability in the here and now; BNSF does as well but looks longer term. A business school professor would say both are perfectly legitimate ways of running a railroad. What I wonder is whether one is better than the other. Or to be blunt: has Union Pacific backed itself into a corner?

The numbers are interesting. Since 2000, UP's carload business (that's everything but intermodal, coal, and autos) fell 2.7 percent. But BNSF's carload traffic rose 23.7 percent. That's an astounding deviation, largely driven by the pricing policies I just discussed. Coal: both railroads peaked in 2008. In the following eight years, UP's coal loadings fell 50 percent, BNSF's just 29 percent. Intermodal: BNSF held a small lead in 2000, a much larger one in 2016. BNSF first passed Union Pacific in total loads in 2004, and last year carried 16 percent more traffic.

Never bet against Union Pacific, because year after year it still brings home more operating income than its rival. This reflects both its emphasis on high rates and the traffic base it enjoys, meaning you earn more per car of chemicals (UP) than per container carried (BNSF). Still, I wonder if there's a tipping point. In other words, both railroads have their high fixed costs. The more business that goes over the rails, the less each car accrues of those costs. BNSF spreads its fixed costs over more and more traffic, UP over less and less. You'd think these trends cannot continue without BNSF's gaining a decided cost advantage over its rival and therefore the ability to underprice the other railroad, with huge consequences.

Today, if you believe in a growing business, it's advantage BNSF Railway. But UP still comes home with that bigger pot of gold. So the battle for supremacy in the West continues.

November 2017 Trains

PART II

TRAVELS AROUND TRAINS

I CANNOT IMAGINE LIKING TRAINS and railroads and not wanting to be on and around them. Can you recall the anticipation of riding trains as a kid, followed of course by the thrill of the experience? Speaking for myself, the anticipation and the enjoyment remain just as great today as they did decades ago. These stories reflect those experiences, and you might be interested in how some of them came about.

Just before I retired in 2009 from editing a magazine about money, Jim Wrinn at *Trains* asked if I wanted to write a monthly column for him. I wasn't sure. A column is really an opinion piece, and doing these well is an art form quite different from other forms of writing. As it happened, I was about to ride Amtrak from Los Angeles to Chicago. Could I write a personal, column-length (950 words) account of that journey? That was the genesis of "The Cocoon of a Long-Distance Train." The piece, written as a sort of experiment for an audience of one—myself—worked well enough that I accepted Jim's offer and later published the account.

There are lots of reasons, I suppose, that people want to write for *Trains*. The big inducement for me was simple: in reporting stories for the magazine, I got to do things that I would otherwise never, ever get to do. As I explained to more than one railroad executive: "This is *Trains*. Its stories need to have the smell of diesel exhaust wafting off the pages. That's why I need to ride your fastest freight train." I wasn't being entirely disingenuous; putting the look and feel of real-life railroading into a business article has a way of bringing it to life. I enjoyed these special occasions so much I'd decide what forbidden pleasure

I wanted to partake and then concoct a story proposal that would permit me to live my dream. "Pencil-Whipping Train 101" appeared in 2007 as a sidebar to a long piece on Florida East Coast Railway. But the real reason I undertook the feature story was to ride train 101. Exhibit B is "No Place for Man or Beast . . . or Train." In 2008, I undertook to write about Canadian railroading in winter. My laboratory was Canadian Pacific Railway, and most of that cover story concerned CP's difficult and endlessly fascinating crossing of the Selkirk range of mountains in British Columbia, where if a runaway train doesn't kill you, an avalanche just may. But before going there, CP treated me to a February trip by freight train over the Canadian Shield, alongside Lake Superior. The weather quickly turned from overcast in Thunder Bay, Ontario, into a full-scale blizzard—a great experience and one owed entirely to representing *Trains*.

I'll share the ultimate example of building a story around once-in-a-lifetime experiences. I made a list of all the you-can't-do-this places I wanted to see and things I wanted to do on Amtrak's Northeast Corridor. They included riding in the cab of a *Metroliner* from Washington to New York, standing over the shoulder of the train dispatcher in Penn Station during rush hour, visiting the key interlocking towers (such as Zoo Tower in Philadelphia), touring the subbasement of Penn Station, and dodging passenger trains on a lowly local freight. I gave the list to Amtrak and said I wanted to do all these things. Lo and behold, my wish was granted, and from that came perhaps my most fun experience ever writing for *Trains*, a story called "The Corridor You Seldom See (Amtrak from the Inside Out)," published in March 1985. The piece "New York City, Then" is adapted from that story. Three decades later, remembering the enjoyment of reporting that article, I did it again for *Trains*, and from that feature story you can read "New York City, Now."

For a couple of these pieces, I can thank my globe-trotting wife, Catherine. "The Ladies of Cork Are Aghast" is the result of having time on my hands in Ireland while accompanying Cathie on one of her business trips. The piece was doubly fun to compose because I got to write a limerick, which of course is a form of Irish humor. Another trip as a corporate spouse got me to Argentina and a not-so-pleasant encounter with that country's downtrodden overnight passenger trains. "The Train to Cordoba" became, almost literally, a trip down the blind side of railroading, and I got my revenge by writing about it.

Do I have a favorite passenger train? Yes, indeed, the *Canadian*, which takes four nights and most of four days going between Toronto and Vancouver. I like it for the scenery, the variety of meals, the people I meet, the busy freight railroad it traverses, and the beautiful, streamliner-era cars now in their seventh decade but looking like new. I try to ride this train twice a year, and invariably these trips become the fodder for magazine columns or online blogs. "My Prestigious Experience" and "The Late, Late Train" recount two such journeys that I still remember fondly.

I get almost as much enjoyment following a railroad in my Dodge Durango and seeing what happens as I do riding the trains themselves. For years my favorite place to hang out was between Richmond, Virginia, and Rocky Mount, North Carolina. CSX Transportation squeezed three dozen passenger and freight trains a day over those 121 miles of mostly single-track railroad. Anything could happen, and it usually did. In "Where Bad Things Happen to Good Trains," I pay tribute to the dozens of days and nights spent prowling the North End Sub, as it's called. Alas, the North End is not half as busy nowadays.

By 2011 I was writing blogs on TrainsMag.com about my encounters with railroads and railroaders. Want to know about a railroad less than a mile long that employs but two people and makes money? "Best Little Railroad in Effingham" came about because I asked an off-the-cuff question of a friend as we drove through central Illinois. Before I knew it, I was being introduced to its owner and then given a royal tour of the property. How many railroads have you ridden from end to end in five minutes? In my lifetime, one.

Lastly, a word about the Buckingham Branch Railroad. In 2005 while train watching on CSX, I came to Doswell, Virginia, where the Washington-Florida main line crosses the original Richmond-Cincinnati route, I spotted in the yard two old GP-7 switchers with the words "Buckingham Branch" stenciled across their flanks.

Buckingham *what*, I asked myself? When I became sufficiently obsessed with this upstart railroad a few years later, I wrote its owner, Bob Bryant, and asked if I could come visit him in southern Virginia and learn the story behind the oddball name. Bob said sure. Out of that trip came a feature story for *Trains* from which "Night Train to Nowhere" was crafted for this book. I hope you enjoy it as much as I did riding that little train all night long.

—〰—

FIFTEEN

THE COCOON OF
A LONG-DISTANCE TRAIN

LEAVING VICTORVILLE LAST NIGHT, THE conductor on Amtrak 4 announced over the PA that there had been an earthquake in California's Mojave Desert east of Barstow, near Ludlow. Richter 5.5. Your train would run at restricted speed until all track and signals were inspected, he said. That was fine with you. On short notice, you'd flown to LA on business that Friday, blown 30,000 Amtrak Guest Rewards points for a deluxe bedroom, and didn't give a damn when you got to Chicago. The last thing you remembered, lying in that big lower bed Friday night, was how nice a ride you got loping past Daggett and Newberry at 20 mph.

You awaken at 7:00, wondering where you are. In a few minutes, the conductor makes her first morning announcement, revealing you are 15 minutes shy of Flagstaff, Arizona, and an hour late. You try in your head to solve the equation: If you lost 60 minutes running 20 mph on an 80-mph railroad, how long did you plod along at restricted speed? But it's too early in the day for that mind bender. After a breakfast of bacon and eggs that tastes as if it had been cooked an hour ago (because it had been), you return to your room. There's work to do: tape a baton-shaped antenna to the window, hook it to a Motorola Maxtrac radio and the radio to your laptop, and fire up ATCS Monitor software.

Your ATCS kit gives you a dispatcher's view of the railroad. For about 15 miles in both directions, you see where the trains are and how

The Moonshiner Duo entertains passengers in the observation lounge of the *Canadian*, in 2012. Of such experiences as this are cocoons made. *Fred W. Frailey*

signals and switches are lined. You tune your scanner to AAR channel 72 and open a timetable to the Seligman Subdivision.

BNSF Railway has reported significant declines in traffic. Tell that to the crews out here. Every 15 minutes a westbound freight flashes by on the south track. And the eastbounds? Leaving Gallup, New Mexico, your *Southwest Chief* soon catches up with an empty grain train headed back to Iowa, and you creep from one approach signal to another. Finally, the dispatcher has a chance to run you around it between West Grants and East Grants.

Pretty soon, you're catching more approach signals. So back you go to the south track at McCartys, New Mexico, to overtake two eastbound double-stack trains between there and Laguna, where two westbounds wait for you to cross back over and get out of their space. And at the next crossovers, you do yet another runaround.

You glance at your watch. Barely 11:00. But it's noon somewhere, so go ahead, order a bloody mary from the snack bar. You open the new Michael Connelly novel. But his Harry Bosch detective thriller is no match for what's outside the window. You try counting the times you've ridden past these red cliffs and finally, lost in the memories, give up.

Albuquerque, New Mexico. In at 12:33 and out at 1:16. You're startled at the sight of the inbound engineer climbing down from the P42 locomotive with a bag of golf clubs slung over his back. By the miracle of padded schedules, you're just 21 minutes late leaving.

You play a mind game called "Where Will the Trains Meet?" A call to Julie, the automated agent, reveals that Amtrak 3, the westbound *Southwest Chief*, is dead on time. Were your train doing as well, you'd probably have met in Glorieta Pass, at Cañoncito, New Mexico, the first siding east of Lamy. Now Lamy, which is the station stop for the state capital in Santa Fe, looks like a cinch for the meet. When you show up, 25 minutes late, train 3 is entering the siding. That was too easy.

But guess what? You won't be able to play that game again. From here to somewhere east of La Junta, Colorado, 280-plus miles, there will be no trains on this Saturday except Amtrak 3 and 4. Empty country, empty railroad. Shortly before reaching Albuquerque, you separated from BNSF's freight line and won't rejoin it until about the time you wake up tomorrow, entering Kansas City. As your train leaves Lamy, the dispatcher issues two track warrants that will get it all the way, unopposed, to La Junta.

You gather your novel and make yourself comfortable in the Sightseer Lounge. Harry Bosch loses again, unable to compete against Apache Canyon, horseshoe curves, jointed rail, and semaphore signals. You spend 90 minutes just staring out the window, alone with your thoughts.

Outside Las Vegas (New Mexico, that is), you decide that it's time to reconnect with the world and call your wife, who is still upset that you didn't fly right back from LA. You say the things that you're supposed to say at such times, all the while thinking to yourself that, given the chance, you'd do it again in a heartbeat.

Harry Bosch gets one more chance to grab your attention in daylight, but the red and brown terrain of the New Mexico desert wins. This is pretty country, in any season. Shoemaker . . . Wagon Mound . . . Springer. All indelible Santa Fe names you first saw in old New Mexico Division timetables. Daylight grows thin on this Saturday in early winter. It's gone entirely by the time you reach Raton. You relax, savoring a martini in your room before making your way to the diner. Your seemingly endless Saturday is winding down after all.

It's been more than 40 years since you first came this way, a happy, unsophisticated college kid riding coach in the *Super Chief–El Capitan* and anticipating that strange place you'd never seen, called California. The whole world was new to you. Much has changed on this railroad and in your life, but the beautiful tableau outside your window today is timeless. Looking out your darkened room east of Lamar, Colorado, you reflect on all this and get a lump in your throat.

You pull up the covers and close your eyes. Life is good.

March 2010 Trains

—⟋⟍—

NO PLACE FOR MAN OR
BEAST . . . OR TRAIN

"THREE DAYS AGO, I TOLD my wife, 'I'm officially tired of winter.'"
It's mid-February, and you're with Don Brosseau, a road manager on
Canadian Pacific's Northern Ontario Service Area, helping him clear
snow from switch points and then shovel the rails of a spur track so that
his Dodge Dakota hi-railer can clear an approaching train.

You feel his pain. Across Ontario's Canadian Shield, winter offers no mountain majesties—just cold, blowing snow. But to really
feel his pain, you would have had to be there three weeks earlier. A
carload freight from Winnipeg had spilled 17 cars between Pays Plat
and Gravel, in one of the region's most inaccessible and inhospitable
locales. Two of those cars, containing paper pulp, lay partially sub-
merged in icy Lake Superior. Roundhouse rumor has it that spikes had
sheared off from the severe cold, causing the derailment on a curve.

"You cannot imagine a worse place to mess up, eleven miles from
a public road in one direction and fourteen in the other, and right
beside Lake Superior," he says. "Conditions were horrific. The temperature varied between four and third-one below zero Fahrenheit,
and the wind chill at night was sixty-two below, with a mist that froze
on your skin."

Brosseau waits a moment as you begin to feel his pain. "It took us
three full days, working around the clock, to reopen the track, and by
then fifty-six trains were being held. We spent a week working off the

backlog. And we left the cars on the ground, including the two in the lake, to pick up this spring. So did I tell you? Winter sucks."

Yesterday just after noon, under overcast skies, you had stepped aboard eastbound intermodal train 108 (Vancouver–Montreal) at Thunder Bay, headed for the next crew change at Schreiber on the Nipigon Sub. Before long, the flakes appear. The farther east you go, the more intense the storm, until you're in a whiteout.

"There's Lake Superior," says the engineer Bob Woodruff, pointing to the right as you pass Nipigon, the last settlement of any size you'll see for the next 60 miles. But all you see is a curtain of white. Remarks the conductor Laurence McParland: "January was really bad. We had lots of stalls on the hills." But the two railroaders you're with aren't complaining. "Winter? I like it," McParland says.

You pass the scene of that derailment. It looks so desolate, like a battlefield after opposing armies have buried their dead and moved on. Lumber juts from one wrecked car like pickup sticks held in a child's hand. All the time, snow blows against the windshield of AC4400CW 8514.

Your train creeps into Schreiber to change crews. Another crew is going on duty to take two light engines to Terrace Bay, the next siding east, where train 220 (Winnipeg–Toronto) has been marooned for four days. The storm is still blowing as you catch a ride to supper.

The next morning, bright and cloudless, you're picked up by Brosseau. He drives to a road crossing at milepost 78 (one of relatively few on the Heron Bay Subdivision, between Schreiber and White River) to put his Dakota on the rails. Then you head west.

"This is the summit—the controlling grade of the entire service area," he tells you. "The grade is 1.3 percent, and curvature adds to the rolling resistance. But if you make it here, you'll get to White River."

A lot of trains aren't making it. Last winter at this time, Brosseau says, two trains had stalled on the grade. But this winter, thirty. In fact, the day before, Winnipeg–Toronto train 222 couldn't get over the hill, and that crew with the light engines went to rescue it instead of train 220, which is still standing on the main track—its fifth day without locomotives—when you go around it at Terrace Bay through the siding.

Still and all, Canadian Pacific gets by during winter on its busy transcontinental route across the Canadian Shield. It easily sees two dozen trains a day. Brosseau darts from siding to siding on the authority of Track Occupancy Permits issued by the train controller, or dispatcher. At practically every one, you either meet an opposing train or are overtaken. By the time you get to Thunder Bay, it's late afternoon of a long day. You're just a visitor, but by now you really do feel Brosseau's pain.

December 2008 Trains

SEVENTEEN

THE LADIES FROM CORK ARE AGHAST

WHEN FRITZ PLOUS LEARNS I am in Dublin, he emails at once that I should go to Limerick Junction, a rail crossing about 120 miles southwest of the capital, on the line to Cork. "It's a station where four railway routes cross in the form of a hollow square," he says. "There's a set of platforms on each of the four sides and, I believe, a set of foot bridges to allow passengers to cross the tracks and reach the connecting platforms. Nothing else like it in the world (just like Chicago Union Station's double-stub track layout)."

I think to myself, now that would be a sight to behold. As it turns out, I have all the time in the world, and this explains why, on a rainy, chilly summer afternoon in Ireland, I find myself almost alone at Limerick Junction.

The last time I'd been in Ireland was 18 years ago. I took a train to Cork and back, passing Limerick Junction twice, and don't recall a thing about the station. I do remember that the Irish Railways (IR) cars were old and a bit gone to seed, like Amfleet cars, in fact. The entire Irish rail infrastructure seemed to be moldering.

Well, much has changed. Ireland has invested prodigiously in its railway. With a capital improvement budget of half a billion Euros a year, IR has virtually replaced its passenger train fleet while opening dormant routes, particularly on the island's west coast.

Armed with this bare body of information, off I go to Dublin's Heuston Station. The noon train to Cork is advertised as having first-class seating and a dining car. When I can find neither on Platform

7, I'm told by the woman supervising loading of the train that it had just been downsized. So I find a seat in a three-car, all-coach DMU (diesel multiple unit) train on which every seat is occupied by people or backpacks. Soon we are off.

Amtrak would be smart to invest in train sets like these. The new DMU trains range up to eight cars in length. They are comfortable, smooth riding, quiet, and fast. I clock my train doing 90 mph, and the driver (engineer) tells me when I reach Limerick Junction that parts of the line are authorized to 100. "I'd like to do better," he says, waiting for his signal to depart.

Anyway, on the 90-minute trek, I review Andrew Dow's recent article in *Trains* about Irish Railways. In it, he had this to say about my destination:

> Writer E.L. Ahrons memorably described the junction as "a sort of four-sided Irish triangle, the chief geometrical property of which is that the longest way around is the shortest way there." This came about because the junction was a flat crossing of north-south and east-west lines, and the single station platform was placed on the west arm. For trains traveling on the east-west line this was adequate, but trains traveling on the north-south line had to either back into the station on one of the curves between the lines, or to run out backward and then run forward on its own line.

While interesting, this description does not seem half as alluring as that provided by Fritz Plous. So which is the real Limerick Junction? On the PA system, my stop is announced, so I get up, prepared to find out. We clomp over an at-grade crossing of the Galway–Limerick–Waterford line and brake shortly thereafter to a stop.

What am I doing here? I wonder. This can't be Limerick Junction! But yes, it is, and obviously that "four-sided Irish triangle" described above had gotten straightened out in the rebuilding of Irish Railways. Gone (if it was ever there) was any semblance of a track arrangement resembling a giant tic-tac-toe, with parallel tracks far apart. Nor are north-south (Dublin–Cork) trains required to perform any gymnastics to reach the station other than to negotiate a crossover at either end. What exists today is the essence of simplicity: The station sits on the Cork line, half a mile south of the crossing of the other route. West of the crossing, a track peels off from the east-west line to bring trains from Galway and Limerick (the latter about 30 miles west of the namesake junction) to a stub track on the other side of the platform used by Dublin–Cork trains. There are no passenger trains east of Limerick Junction to Waterford.

Needless to say, I'm a bit let down. I enjoy going in search of unlikely stories and accept that some don't work out. At least, I say to myself, the return train to Dublin has first-class seating and a dining car. Well, yes and no. The first-class seats and the dining car are the same thing, but "dining" as defined on Irish Railways is cold sandwiches and coffee that even the cafe cars on Amtrak's short-distance trains beat by a mile. The only luxury is to have the sandwich and coffee brought to your seat, your seat being indistinguishable from a regular coach seat.

When I get back to Heuston Station, the rain has intensified. I am two miles from my hotel and without an umbrella. Still, in the taxi I compose a limerick to commemorate the day. It's not perfect, but neither was my adventure.

The ladies from Cork are aghast.
Their train has arrived at last.
But instead of delay,
they leave right away
as Limerick Junction flies past.

August 15, 2013 TrainsMag.com

EIGHTEEN

CROSSING THE COUNTRY IN A BLUR

ON MAY 6, 1969, I was a 25-year-old newspaper reporter and began the most thrilling train ride of my life, from Chicago to Los Angeles aboard Santa Fe Railway's legendary intermodal train, the Super C, known to crews then as No. 99. Decades have passed, and still nothing quite like this experience has come my way. It's time I shared it with you.

In early 1968, Santa Fe inaugurated this 40-hour, premium-priced piggyback train. The first westbound run set a Chicago–LA speed record of 34 hours, 35 minutes, and 40 seconds that still stands. But the train quickly fell into a funk. In its first year, it typically ran with a single trailer, if it operated at all. In that era, $1,400 was a lot to demand. Then the US Post Office Department, with its deep pockets, came to the rescue. The train began carrying at least a dozen trailers of mail a day. Its future seemed secure.

With that, I begin to scheme. How do I ride this train? I propose to the editor of the Chicago *Sun-Times* Sunday magazine a feature story on what it takes to get a freight train to LA in the same time as the *Super Chief.* He likes it. Santa Fe president John Reed signs off. I show up at 7:00 a.m. at Corwith Yard on a Monday, almost walking on air.

Bob Gehrt, of Santa Fe's Public Relations Department, accompanies me. Bob probably drew the short straw when the decision was made on who would accompany me, but this trip seals a friendship that lasts to this day. His wife, Arline, hands us a tin of cookies she'd baked.

So that we'll not interfere with things, the railroad adds what it calls a "passenger caboose" ahead of the real one. But I'm free to ride the locomotives whenever I wish. In other words, I have the run of this train. Off we go at 8:14 a.m. with 7 flatcars, 12 trailers, and 2 cabooses, hauled by 2 warbonneted U28CGs and 1 U30CG locomotive, giving us an unbelievable 12 horsepower per ton. After clearing metropolitan Chicago at Joliet, we easily reach our maximum speed, 80 mph. At Verona, milepost 71, we wham past the eastbound *Texas Chief* and its four F units at a combined 170 mph.

Crossing the Illinois River, I notice a canoe far below. Three minutes later, we're in Chillicothe, Illinois, for a 60-second crew change. Just by Galesburg, we smell burning brake shoes. The road foreman of engines is in our caboose and radios ahead: "Are we about to reach a crossover?" "What crossover?" "Our air pressure back here is 65 pounds." "We're OK up front." "We've got a busted air hose, then. Stop and we'll take a look."

In a mild rainstorm, I follow the road foreman, Joe Elliott, carrying his spare air hose and a 30-inch wrench. We're under way in seven minutes. But a bit later the brakes go into emergency—another busted hose. Joe uses our last spare hose.

We stop on the outside track of Kansas City Union Station at 3:52 p.m. A switcher adds seven cars of trailers and takes away four. We're moving at 4:31 p.m. At Tower 3 comes No. 100, the eastbound Super C, with 4 locomotives, 12 cars, and caboose. I ride the head end to Wellington, Kansas, which we reach at 9:55 p.m. In five minutes we get a new crew and a big gulp of diesel fuel.

Bob and I are about to attempt sleep in the caboose bunks when, at Mooreland, Oklahoma, a revolving white light indicates a hotbox, and we stop. I drop to the ground as our train is inspected. Mooreland has gone to bed for the night. All I hear is the barking of a solitary dog. In a few minutes' time we are on the move again.

I awaken nearing Largo, New Mexico, between Clovis and Vaughn and sit in the cupola, enjoying a cigarette and sipping cold coffee while Bob contentedly slumbers. Within a few minutes, we slip into the siding at 40 mph, and presently (the siding is 216 cars long) another edition of No. 100 whips past on the main line. We never stopped. I feel goose bumps.

A road foreman of engines boards our passenger caboose at Vaughn with a thermos of coffee and egg sandwiches. To the relief of Bob and me, he knows how to get the stove started on our car, and we begin to thaw out. Then about 50 miles east of Belen, New Mexico, it begins to snow—remember, it's early May! Before you know it, we're in a blizzard running against strong headwinds, our speed slowing to 50 mph. Then just as quickly as the squall began, it ends, the sun comes out, and a warm desert day gets underway.

Two other events stand out from Day 2. First, 12 miles before a crew change in Gallup, New Mexico, our second unit shuts down. We're told a mechanic awaiting us would have 30 seconds to restart locomotive 400. "Then get the hell out of here," the yardmaster adds. But engine 400 won't restart. Therefore, at Winslow, Arizona, what should back against our train but a fourth locomotive, F45 No. 1936. Just as we leave, a mechanic gets 400 restarted, and now our HPT (horsepower per ton) ratio is obscene.

Second, from Needles, California, to Barstow, the dispatcher had given other westbound freights times to clear our train at various sidings on the north track. (Centralized traffic control to permit bidirectional running on both tracks was decades away.) But we are 10 minutes ahead of his estimates. So the operator at lonely Cadiz is kept busy on the radio, relaying new clearing times.

Summit, atop Cajon Pass, 6:13 p.m. San Bernardino and the final crew change, 7:00 p.m. Racing down the Third District in fading light, the road foreman has me run the train for half an hour. We blaze through the LA suburbs at a frightening speed, my whistle blaring with the urgency of a police car siren, and I am thrilled. No. 99 stops at Hobart Yard at 8:29. Trip time: 38 hours, 15 minutes. Gehrt and I are dirty, disheveled, and exhausted. But who cares? After all, it was my trip of a lifetime.

As for the Super C, it lasted but eight years, always dependent on that post office contract. When the contract came up for rebidding in 1976, Union Pacific offered to move the mail for less, and as quickly as it burst upon the scene in 1968, this train quietly vanished. Nobody has succeeded since in running a freight train so swiftly.

November 2011 Trains

NINETEEN

ODE TO A COACH YARD

TALK ABOUT PERSONAL RESPONSIBILITY: JOSEPH Pepitone's Amtrak business card reads, "General Foreman, Trains 87/88 'The Silver Meteor' Sunnyside Yard." On this August day, No. 88 is 27 minutes late into New York's Pennsylvania Station from Florida, and Pepitone does his first walk-through of the 14 cars even before their passengers ascend the escalators from Track 11. Up ahead, the yard engineer Tom Kubick enters the road locomotive, E60 motor 964, and drills the Tampa mail car onto Track 12, where it will be grabbed by an engine from the west side of the station and placed for unloading on the Diagonal Track. (Mostly, yard crews commandeer whatever road locomotive is available to do this.)

At 12:15 p.m., 45 minutes after arrival, Kubick gets his signal from JO Tower—in reality a hut in the dark bowels of Penn Station—and heads the empty train into the East River runnel for Sunnyside. Within exactly 4 hours, the cars must be washed, switched, cleaned, inspected, repaired, restocked, returned to Penn Station, loaded, and sent back to Florida. It's no small task.

"Working for me I have 6 electricians, 7 carmen, 2 pipefitters, and 18 coach cleaners, and together we handle No. 81, No. 183, No. 285 and then 87–88," Pepitone explains from a vestibule as Kubick pulls the consist through Sunnyside's car washer on a loop track at 2 mph. Coming out of the loop, past the abandoned Railway Express Agency warehouse, it opens up before you—the 33 tracks of this enormous facility.

Sunnyside Yard is not at the height of its glory. In 1955 for the Pennsylvania Railroad, it dispatched 211 sleepers and 57 diners a day on 54 through trains, and in addition serviced the fleet of commuter trains. Today it handles 35 trains in all. On the other hand, despite anything you may have heard over the years, it is *not* lost in a sea of weeds and decay. It is *not* overrun by neighborhood vandals from surrounding Queens. It is *not* a place where employees sleep away the day and send the trains out just as they came in—at least not with Joe Pepitone around.

With the *Silver Meteor* now parked on Track 6, the first order of business is to switch out one 60-seat Amfleet coach for another in the Miami portion of the train. While that's going on, you look about. A wire train sits behind an orange GP9, awaiting assignment. To your left is the *Broadway Limited*, getting a final look-over, and next to that six Metroliner (now called Capitol Liner) multiple-unit cars awaiting that evening's *Valley Forge* to Harrisburg. Intermixed are a couple of New York–Philadelphia Clockers. And to the right, nine other tracks hold both conventional and MU trains belonging to New Jersey Transit.

No. 19, the *Crescent*, leaves for loading at the station. "That's Mr. Claytor's train," remarks the transportation manager Steve Strachan, referring to Amtrak's president. "When all goes will with the *Crescent*, my whole day goes well. When it gets messed up . . ."

By 1:20, the switching is finished, the cars again get electricity from the 964, and work begins in earnest on the *Meteor*. Now Pepitone goes into perpetual motion—looking, testing, asking, answering, cajoling, suggesting, and occasionally fretting.

Today Lillet Walker, his supervisor of car cleaners, has a crew of 11. "They have from 1:30 to 3:15 to get the job done," she explains. Two people will work the three sleepers, five will handle the remaining cars, two will vacuum, one will clean toilets, and one will water the cars outside.

Problems, problems: Pepitone feels the air conditioner's output on Amcoach 25067; it seems weak. "Check that out," he tells an electrician; the unit gets a shot of freon. He dispatches someone to find a replacement cover to a coffeemaker on lounge 3114; none can be found. "We'll cut a cover ourselves and install it next trip," he decides. Another electrician replaces the ballast in a fluorescent light. Two pipe fitters wrestle with a stripped gear in a leg rest on the next-to-last car; they're having trouble removing it.

The *Meteor* is alive with activity. Huge bundles of dirty bedding sit on the platform as sleeping-car attendants store away the replacements. Headrests are torn from coach seats and replaced. Trash is piled on seats and then collected in huge plastic bags. Leg rests are thrown atop seats before vacuuming and then returned to place. Every metal surface gets a wipe down—interiors of the windows, too. The lived-in look fades fast.

Commissary trucks bring crates of food for the diner and two lounges. Cooks stow away new dinner provisions that supplement what came up from Miami the day before—an additional 24 short ribs of beef, 12 vegetable lasagnas, 48 chickens, 20 snapper filets, and 30 strip steaks.

"Car cleaners are leaving," Ms. Walker announces over the PA system at 3:15. The pipe fitters finally disassemble the broken leg rest and begin installing a new gear. Pepitone, now at the opposite end of the train, sends someone to check on their progress. "Goose them a bit—we're running out of time," he adds. He makes a final walk-through, testing each toilet and then reading the defect report kept on every car to satisfy himself that all reported problems have been addressed.

"Pipe fitters are off," comes the word over the PA. "Eighty-seven's ready to go!" trumpets a relieved Pepitone in reply. He gets off, too, as the train heads for Manhattan at 3:30—clean, pretty, and well groomed . . . as Mr. Claytor would want it.

July 1985 Trains

TWENTY

BY TRAIN TO THE END OF
THE EARTH

IT'S BEEN 42 YEARS SINCE the Denver & Rio Grande Western (D&RGW) sold its magnificent, 64-mile line over Cumbres Pass to the states of Colorado and New Mexico and got out of narrow-gauge railroading. And yes, it has taken me that long to get to Antonito, Colorado, and savor the successor railroad these states created, the three-foot-gauge Cumbres & Toltec Scenic (C&TS)—"Pride of the Rockies," it calls itself, with some justification. The C&TS has had its ups and downs, about once a decade being visited by the economic or managerial Perils of Pauline. But it's still here, waiting for me to end my procrastination.

I get to Antonito (30 miles south of the larger city of Alamosa) the afternoon before my trip west on No. 215 and wait for the passage of its eastbound counterpart five miles east of town, in the sagebrush on a right-of-way road. I can hear the exhaust of Mikado 488 before the train comes into view half a mile away. What a gorgeous sight, that dinky little locomotive and its seven trailing cars. I instantly think of a similar pugnacious narrow-gauge train in Patagonia that brought the writer Paul Theroux to the end of his rail adventures, from Boston to southern Argentina, more than a third of a century ago.

Amazingly, this railroad still operates by timetable and train order, the timetable setting the meeting point of trains 215 and 216 at Osier, where the trains pause an hour or longer for lunch.

The view from the rear at the Lava loop as the narrow-gauge Cumbres & Toltec Scenic disappears into the San Juan Mountains . . . You may as well be on Mars. *Fred W. Frailey*

We leave Antonito the next morning two minutes after the scheduled 10:00 a.m. departure because half a dozen late arrivals run to the station just as the engineer whistles off. "Stop the train," the conductor sighs over the radio. These folks bring the passenger count to 81. Behind 488 today are a coach with a wheelchair lift, three coaches, a gondola for passengers desiring an open-air experience, a table car, and a first-class car, which is where I occupy chair number five. Like the original cars used by C&TS in 1970, these passenger cars appear to have started life as boxcars; at any rate, they sure don't come shot welded from Budd Manufacturing Company.

My one regret about this visit is that I forget to reread (or bring with me) the story authored by Philip R. Hastings in the April 1956 issue of *Trains*, "Into the Freezing Darkness," his account of riding D&RGW freights from Alamosa to Chama, New Mexico, and back in April 1955. Hastings is justly celebrated for his photography, but his haunting account of this journey is a journalistic masterpiece, one of the best narratives ever published by *Trains*. If you own the DVD *Trains Magazine: The Complete Collection, 1940–2010*, look this one up.

I stand on the rear platform with the uniformed trainman as Antonito fades into the distance below us. "Well, 18 and a half miles an hour," he said, having timed from milepost 283 to 284. "That's the best we'll do today." A few moments later you feel the train slow as it reaches the start of the grade. We are in high desert country, surrounded by sagebrush and not much else. If there is grass to support livestock grazing, I can't see it.

The first of many hairpin turns takes us around the Lava (New Mexico) loop. I snap a photo as the train retreats from the unused water tower. By and by we leave the desert and climb into forested mountains, the heart of the San Juan range. Our train hugs the high ridges; far below us flows the Rio de Los Pinos, looking tiny and dry. I try many times (it's hard, actually) to imagine it is 1949, and I am a Colorado businessman heading from Denver overnight by Pullman to Alamosa and then by café-parlor car on D&RGW's *San Juan Express* to Durango. Going back ever further, in 1919 Antonito to Chama took three and a half hours. Subtract the time we'll spend eating today, and it takes five hours. How you could have covered this territory so much faster then eludes me.

I cannot begin to describe how removed from civilization this railroad is today. From the time we leave Antonito until sometime after lunch, I see not a sign of human habitation other than preserved railroad structures once lived in by track workers. At Sublette, population today zero, almost two hours into the trip, we stop so that 488 can top off its water from a standpipe. Then off we go into nowhere again, crossing the Colorado–New Mexico border three more times that morning; if I count correctly, we change states eleven times on this journey. After Sublette comes Mud Tunnel, Phantom Curve, and Rock Tunnel.

At 1:00 o'clock, 15 minutes behind the timetable schedule, train 215 rounds a curve and before us stands Osier, eastbound train 216 already there, its locomotive gently sending a curl of steam into the air. Osier has a strange effect on me. It had once been a small community, and a 1919 employee timetable of mine indicates it had a depot and agent. C&TS built a two-story structure there some years ago to serve as a lunch facility for its trains. The building nicely blends into its surroundings. After eating, I photograph the older structures (including what had been a rooming house), climb a hillside, and look around the treeless landscape. Nowheresville. Leaving aside the fact that a dirt road allows the kitchen employees to reach this place, the emptiness and isolation of Osier today is overwhelming. The only time I have had a similar feeling is driving the Forest Service road east from Winter Park, Colorado, built on the right-of-way of the original railroad route above Moffat Tunnel and looking down on Yankee Doodle Lake. At times like these, you leave the world behind. Believe it or not, the emotional experience causes me to tear up.

We've been climbing all day. After Osier, the ascent continues, but now below us are grasslands, cattle being grazed, and occupied homes. Right at the summit, 10,015 feet above sea level, we whistle for Colorado Highway 17 (which also goes through Antonito, I might add) and come to a stop at Cumbres, for a brake test and a setup of brake retainers, which maintain a constant braking application no matter what the engineer does. Our grade thus far has been on the order of 2 percent, going up. From Cumbres to Chama, 15 miles, it's a constant 4 percent descent, and do we ever feel it, hear it, and smell it.

It's as steep a mountain grade as you'll find anywhere in the United States today (short of a cog railway), but with Highway 17 almost always within sight, it is neither as desolate nor as romantic as it had been, in the middle of Nowheresville. I miss Nowheresville.

At 4:20, about 15 minutes late (but who cares?), we come to a stop in Chama. The feeling I have, rolling slowly through the former Rio Grande yard, is of coming upon a 1930s movie set. Here, a coal tipple so old it must predate the railroad. There, a string of converted boxcars that probably constituted the initial fleet of C&TS passenger coaches. And everywhere, antique boxcars, refrigerator cars, and cattle cars, looking as if being readied for yet another movie filmed on the premises. Several steam locomotives that appear to be in good working order await their awakening.

Before boarding the bus to take me back to Antonito, I look up at engine 488. Two men are peering out from the cab. I approach them. "Which of you is the fireman?" I ask. The older man on the left, and the least unkempt and disheveled, says he is. "Are you tired by now?" I ask. (These locomotives are hand fired, mind you.) "In about twenty years I'll be," he replies with a broad grin. I snap a photo of them and greet the bus driver.

I hope I have inspired you. Why make my mistake and waste another 42 years? Get thee there, now. Two inexpensive books I recommend are *Saving the Cumbres & Toltec Scenic Railroad* (History Press, 2012), about the post–Rio Grande years and the perils of not-for-profit ownership, and *Ticket to Toltec* (Western Guideways), a mile-by-mile description of the railroad you will experience. But above all else, before you go, read Phil Hastings's piece in *Trains*. It speaks to you through all the decades, better than I ever can.

August 16, 2012 TrainsMag.com

His takeout food in one hand, Florida East Coast engineer Kenny James waves
as train 202 flashes through Palm Bay. His train 101, at right, waits patiently.
Fred W. Frailey

TWENTY ONE

PENCIL-WHIPPING TRAIN 101

BY 11:15 ON THIS THURSDAY morning, Tommy Rountree is becoming concerned. A bear of a man, he's general manager of the northern half of Florida East Coast Railway (FEC). His concern is that the first mile of train 101 is missing. It's on a transfer train somewhere between the CSX intermodal terminal northwest of downtown Jacksonville and FEC's Bowden Yard on the city's south end, and 101 is due to leave in just 45 minutes. The back half of this 10,113-foot intermodal monster is already loaded, inspected, and sitting on the main line. For FEC veterans like Rountree, on-time departures are a matter of both policy and pride.

At 11:25—the last possible moment—a CSX switcher crawls into Bowden with a seemingly endless string of trailers and containers, 22 of them bearing United Parcel Service logos. The pieces quickly come together. An FEC engine takes over, pulls the cut through a crossover, and pushes it against the rear half of 101. Then a hostler attaches two shiny SD70M-2 locomotives, and a brake test begins. By the time engineer Kenny James and conductor Craig Cameron are driven to the front and stow their gear, a carman on lead motor 102 is filling out the brake-test clearance. "101 to dispatcher," James radios, "we're ready to go." Just ahead, a centralized traffic control signal at Sunbeam, the extreme south end of Bowden, blinks to green and their train is moving at 12:05.

The next day's morning report will show train 101 leaving Jacksonville's yard at noon on the dot. This slight time discrepancy is known as "pencil-whipping," and the practice is as old as railroading. As Roun-tree explains: "Well, Sunbeam is about five minutes south of the yard tower."

Every day, two of the railroad's four new SD70s power 101, the pre-mier intermodal run on the railroad. But their 8,600 horses are no match this afternoon, even on flat terrain, for a train that's longer than the eye can see. By 12:30, with the speedometer hovering at 51 mph, James admits defeat. "The best we're going to do," he says, "is 52 or 53. But they'll keep us moving."

The first thing you notice about this train is its ride quality: su-per smooth. It's a credit to concrete ties and the mountain of granite rock they rest on. The second thing you notice is that the right-of-way is littered with old concrete ties recently taken out of the track. The problem, you later learn, is that fasteners used to hold the rail to the ties worked loose and made many ties unusable. So, for the past several years, the railroad has installed a more secure type of fastener and replaced those ties too far gone to accept the replacements.

And the third thing you notice is that for the 70 or so miles beyond St. Augustine (milepost 34), 101 traverses unpopulated, undeveloped land that probably hasn't changed much since Henry Flagler built the railroad more than a century ago. The bottom 80 miles of the FEC will be starkly different this evening, as your train runs a gauntlet of South Florida grade crossings.

You slow to a crawl at Dorena, 55 miles south of Bowden Yard, at 1:20, while an extra intermodal train clears, and again 45 minutes later to let local train 905 out of your way just north of Ormand Beach.

At 2:30, passing the former crew change point of New Smyrna Beach (milepost 125), James takes a break and the conductor, Cameron, sits in the engineer's seat. Like most FEC conductors, Cameron is a qualified engineer. He's also, it turns out, an avid investor in the stock market. "I work as little as possible," Cameron says as he whistles through Edge-water. "I like to trade stocks—day trade." To Cameron, a long-term investment lasts two weeks. "I should have bought Winn-Dixie yes-terday," he says. "It's up 80 cents today."

He and James begin talking about the price of Florida East Coast Industries (FECI) stock, which has been steadily rising this year. Most

FEC train-service employees you meet turn out to own shares of their company, and more than a few of them will soon see their net worth swell when FECI is taken private at a price 30 percent higher than today's.

Past Daytona Beach and New Smyrna Beach, you're back in wilderness. Your favorite spot passes quickly—those few miles north of Titusville (milepost 154) when the tracks run close to the Inland Waterway and far from the rest of civilization. But then you pass Jay Jay and a connection with the NASA Railway. You round a curve and bid good-bye to solitude as US Highway 1 swoops overhead from the west and brings you into urban Florida to stay.

Four hours into the trip, passing Pineda and the halfway mark, the radio comes alive. "FEC dispatcher to train 101. I've got you lined for the siding at Palm Bay. You may be there for a while. I've got a small situation with 206." His train tucked inside Palm Bay, Cameron shuts down the SD70s while James walks to a convenience store on US 1 for some food. The wait for train 206 to set out a disabled boxcar lasts 40 minutes. Then it slams by you at full speed with the railroad's other two SD70s.

Delayed ahead of you by 206 was train 109, with empty rock cars, which left Jacksonville at 10:00 a.m. Now it's only six to eight miles in front, and the dispatcher says you'll go around it at Fort Pierce (milepost 241), which you do at 6:00 o'clock. You ask James how late 101 is now. "Oh, we're about on schedule," he replies. "Don't worry about it."

In fading light, 101 blares for the Hobe Sound road crossing, cuts through a state park, crosses the Jupiter River drawbridge, and finally, at 7:30, ties up eight lanes of traffic on Okeechobee Boulevard, bringing downtown West Palm Beach to a standstill.

You have reached South Florida.

Wayne Blalock, the railroad's general manager for the south end, will tell you the next morning that FEC crosses 400 streets between West Palm and Miami. After listening to James sound motor 102's whistle almost continuously the next hour and a half, you won't argue the point. Lake Worth, Boynton Beach, Delray Beach, Boca Raton, Deerfield Beach, Pompano Beach, Fort Lauderdale, and North Miami all go by in a blur of automobile headlights, crossing gates, nearby shopping malls, and occasional industry spurs. South of downtown Fort Lauderdale on the adjacent track, local 970 works the vest-pocket intermodal yard, building tonight's UPS train 224, which will depart (count on it) at 11:00 o'clock.

At 9:00, passing North Miami, James radios ahead to Hialeah Yard. "Keep 'em coming," he's told by the yardmaster. You enter Hialeah's four-track intermodal facility 23 minutes later, where northbound UPS shooter 226 is being loaded for an 11:00 o'clock launch. By the time the rear of your train is in the terminal, your locomotives have made a 180-degree turn on a balloon track and are headed back to Jacksonville. You finally stop at 9:37 p.m., 22 minutes late.

You can't pencil-whip 22 minutes to read on time. But considering the size of the train you pulled and the hit you took at Palm Bay waiting on 206, you mean every word of it when you shake James's hand and say, "Good run, Kenny!"

October 2007 Trains

TWENTY TWO

I PLEAD THE FIFTH

WE ALL KNOW ABOUT "TAKING the Fifth." It's our right under the Fifth Amendment to the US Constitution not to be compelled to testify against ourselves. In other words, a traffic court cannot force you to admit driving 60 mph in a 45-mph zone or to dumping your garbage at the door to City Hall. That amendment has another, less-well-known clause, which says government cannot take away our property without just compensation. Lawyers know this as the "Takings Clause." The Takings Clause came to mind the other day as I rode Amtrak's *Empire Builder* from Seattle to Chicago. I'll get to my point, but first the experience.

Our eastbound *Builder* was more than two hours late leaving Seattle. The reason was the four-hours'-late arrival of No. 7, its westbound counterpart, and the need to turn, clean, and restock the equipment before boarding passengers for the run back to Chicago.

The next morning I began to understand what had befallen No. 7 and practically every other recent edition of this train, including our own. BNSF Railway across the northern tier of states is busier than ever in its history. It is seeing 50 trains a day on what is predominantly a single-track railroad in Washington, Idaho, Montana, and western North Dakota. And the *Empire Builder* is being nicked to death despite good dispatching by the host railroad.

Not once did I observe our train take siding for a BNSF freight. Still, we suffered from following freights on approach signals until they could clear to let us by, waiting briefly for opposing freights to appear and take siding, or halting while a train longer than the siding it occupied snaked its way out. To be sure, we were also slowed by "heat orders" necessitated by 100-degree afternoon temperatures and by the fact that our train had to be recrewed short of Minot, North Dakota; because our new Amtrak crew wasn't qualified west of that town, we waited on a BNSF pilot to ferry us for 40 miles.

All of this did terrible things to our schedule keeping. By the third morning, as the train approached Devils Lake, North Dakota, we were more than eight hours late. (The next day's eastbound *Builder* was even later.) But imagine what the *Empire Builder* does to BNSF's freights every day. The Amtrak Improvement Act of 1973 reads: "Except in an emergency, intercity passenger trains operated by or on behalf of [Amtrak] shall be accorded preference over freight trains in the use of any given line of track, junction, or crossing." BNSF appears totally committed to obedience of this law, but doing so devours the capacity of this route. It's not just that freights give way; whizzing along at 79 mph versus 55 or 60 for the freights, the *Empire Builder* eats capacity as if it were two or three freights. Six high-priority Z-class freights prowl the northern Transcon every day, and I don't think a single one of them that I observed was moving as we went by. One Z train was sandwiched between two stopped manifest trains, all waiting for our *Builder*.

Obviously, Amtrak pays BNSF for the right to run trains over the freight railroad. But whatever it pays is but a fraction of the cost in delays to its own trains incurred by BNSF. Were the northern Transcon double tracked all the way, these delays would obviously be minimized. But at $4 million or more a mile, double tracking consumes capital like a dry sponge, and it's not Amtrak's capital, either.

So now to my point: Isn't it fair to say that Amtrak, which the US Supreme Court in 2015 decreed to be an arm of government, is confiscating the property (track capacity) of host railroads? And if it is, shouldn't the freight railroads be fairly compensated for the delays to their freights caused by the loss of this capacity? Try as I might to say otherwise, I am forced to answer yes to both questions.

A very senior railroad attorney tells me that as a law student at the time of the 1973 legislation about priority for Amtrak trains, he wrote the Association of American Railroads to urge it to file suit based on the Takings Clause. The AAR obviously did not, perhaps fearing public backlash. Maybe that's still the case. But back the freight railroads against the wall hard enough, and such litigation is bound to occur. I almost wish it would. The grand bargain that created Amtrak in 1970 required railroads to pay millions to be relieved of their passenger train responsibilities. The 1973 law giving Amtrak trains priority wasn't part of that deal.

The way things are now, with most routes used by Amtrak fully subscribed by freight trains, it's almost impossible for Amtrak to even suggest running additional passenger trains. The host railroads aren't about to let the reliability of their freight services become even more untenable. So the growth of rail passenger traffic outside the Northeast Corridor is practically nil. On the other hand, if we dealt with this issue honestly (as I think our Constitution requires) and actually paid for the capacity that passenger trains consume, the host railroads would be more open to adding Amtrak frequencies.

For me, none of this is easy to say. I look forward to being aboard passenger trains as much as or more today than I did as a kid. Maybe, if Amtrak were compelled to pay for the track capacity the *Empire Builder* devours, there would be no *Empire Builder*. But arrivals four and eight hours late, which seems to be the rule today, are not acceptable, either. We need better solutions than beating freight railroads over the head.

November 2018 Trains

A Prestige Class bedroom by day. By night, a queen-sized Murphy bed extends from the window (left) to the wall (right). The 1 percenters love it. *Fred W. Frailey*

TWENTY THREE

—⁐—

MY PRESTIGIOUS EXPERIENCE

HALF A DOZEN YEARS AGO, the folks at VIA Rail Canada asked what was needed to attract the 1 percent crowd to their flagship, the Toronto-to-Vancouver *Canadian*. That is, the 1 percent of us with the most money. The 1 percenters can have about any travel experience they want. Back then, the *Canadian* wasn't attracting this gang. VIA decided to create something that would cost the big bucks but leave people thinking they got something really impressive in exchange. Thus, was born, in 2014, the Prestige Class.

The reaction of railfans to Prestige has been monodimensional. Does this mean, they asked, we can't ride in the Park car, the train's signature sleeper-bar lounge-dome observation car at the end of the trains? VIA's people wrestled with this question, veering this way and that, but finally concluded that making the Park car the exclusive playground of the Prestige customers wasn't worth the fight. Besides, there always seems to be, in any season, room for everyone who wants to be there.

As for the Prestige Class experience, I've been slowly tilting from disinterest to ambivalence to keen desire to experience it myself. And now I have, on my own dime no less, making me a 1 percenter.

Before I answer the question you all must be asking, let me describe what you get as a Prestige customer. VIA took eight little-used Chateau-class sleepers and four Park-class observation cars and remade them into something rather unique in North America. Each of the Chateau cars has but six suites (plus a cubbyhole for the attendant, who usually sleeps in a vacant double bedroom elsewhere). Each Park car has one suite for the disabled and one other identical to those in the Chateau cars (in addition to the lounge, dome, and so forth).

I carefully computed the size of each suite in square footage and then cluelessly threw away the paper that contained the numbers and gave away the book that contained the information the numbers are based on. But each suite is almost twice the size of a double bedroom. It has an enclosed bathroom and its own shower. Windows are super-sized. By day, a leatherette divan runs across two sides of the room. By night, a queen-size Murphy bed comes down, giving room enough to let two people play footsie. There's a fridge that your attendant will stock with the booze and wine you desire. When you get bored, you can watch movies on the flat-screen monitor. In the Park car dome, the attendant will entertain you from time to time with stories about the train that are largely true. As with all the folks in the regular sleeping cars, your meals come with the ticket, and no two menus will ever be the same. Oh, lest I forget: when you check in, you get two taxi vouchers to take you to the restaurant of your choice and get you back to board the train that evening.

And what will impress Amtrak customers most of all, in four and a half days I heard not one single squeak signifying loose doors, appliances, and so forth.

So, you're dying to know: Is it worth Can$8,085—approximately US$6,200 when I made the booking—one way to enjoy all this? (Bear in mind that's the price whether there is one of you in the room or two.) And my answer is, silly boy, of course not. But doggone, it *is* one fine experience. I lucked out and got the one regular suite in the Park car, and I've never been so genuflected toward in my life. The staff does everything but lay palm leaves on the floor in front of you. "Would you like something to drink, Mr. Frailey?" I'm asked in the dome. "Are you ready for your room to be made up?" "May we leave the rest of the bottle of that wine in your room?" I wish I had asked, impromptu, for a locomotive ride; it would probably have been instantly arranged by the train director, the bosses in Montreal never being the wiser.

I asked every VIA employee I saw how the Prestige service is selling, and the answer is, very well. It began with one Chateau car and is now at two, which is the maximum available during the warm season when the train runs triweekly. On my train, all 14 rooms were occupied. And based on my experiences aboard luxury cruises, I think Prestige patrons get an experience comparable to what the 1 percent would expect at sea—the whole thing seems very cruise competitive, down even to the price.

Looking at this new service another way, it's no coincidence that the Canadian government's subsidy of this train has shrunk by $10 million since the introduction of the Prestige Class. Each of the 72 departures east and west during June through August, when Prestige is normally sold out, brings in more than $100,000 of Prestige revenue from people who probably weren't riding the *Canadian* previously.

The reason it wasn't worth $8,085 to me is simply that I don't ride this train for the soft downy pillows and obsequious treatment. I ride it to look at the mountains and prairies and lakes outside the train and the living, breathing freight railroad we share tracks with, Canadian National. I can enjoy all of this whether I ride Prestige or book a bargain-basement upper berth in the section part of a Manor-series sleeper (and by the way, the mattress in an upper berth is half again thicker than that on a Prestige bed).

All that said, I enjoyed the heck out of the Prestige experience. It was fun having all that room, all that attention . . . and also all that privacy.

We got the usual handling from Canadian National on VIA No. 2, the eastbound *Canadian*. That is, we took the siding for 95 percent of the opposing freight trains we met. This has always been standard practice. So the variable becomes this: Is Canadian National having a relatively good day, its freights somewhat close to schedule and running without incident? If so, we'll get a break and the opposing train will be waiting for us when we get to a siding or will pass as we drift through the siding. Or is CN royally screwed up? This can be the case over much of the winter season, as storms disrupt operations and bone-chilling temperatures inhibit airbrakes from releasing on the two- and three-mile long freights. If CN is in trouble, the *Canadian* is in double trouble. Freights won't be waiting for us when we get to the meeting point, and delays to our train multiply. On such occasions the *Canadian* gets to the other end 14 or so hours late.

Canadian National was in fine fettle for my trip in 2016. By day three, we were a mere two and a half hours late leaving Armstrong, Ontario, on the CN Caramat Subdivision, 244 miles. The *Canadian's* schedule allots almost eight hours for this distance, so you'd think we'd make up a good chunk of time. Here is what really happened:

We make flag stops at Auden (mile 192), Nakina (mile 132), Caramat (mile 78), and Hillsport (mile 42). Figure a delay of ten minutes each stop, including arriving and leaving. That's 40 lost minutes. Then comes the gauntlet of westbounds: intermodal train 105 at Green (mile 226), a long manifest train at Ferland (mile 214), intermodal train 115 at Cavell (mile 147), our westbound counterpart, VIA train 1, at Otterdale (mile 51), and, finally, intermodal 111 at Lennon (mile 6).

Train 111 is a special situation. It leaves Toronto about 1:00 a.m. every morning for Vancouver, mostly with domestic containers, and answers only to the voice of God. It is not to be stopped or even slowed. So figure a 30-minute delay each time we encounter the train, which is roughly every 12 hours. Today, the terminal at Hornpayne, Ontario (mile 0), which has only three usable tracks, is jammed, so we are held at Lennon, the closest siding, for 111 to arrive in Hornpayne, recrew, and depart. For us, this lasts an hour. So instead of making up time across the Caramet Sub, we lose 65 minutes. And that's a good outcome, considering all that went on.

For the record, we reach Toronto Union Station the next day at noon, 2.5 hours late, which for the *Canadian* is the same as ahead of time. A VIA train 2 a couple of trips ahead of us was 14 hours late, and one a trip or two later was reported running 7 hours late.

And my thoughts? Just recounting our trudge across the Caramat makes me want to ride the train again.

October 17 and 24, 2016 TrainsMag.com

—⟋⟍—

TWENTY FOUR

THE LATE, LATE TRAIN

VIA RAIL'S *CANADIAN*, TRAIN 2 from Vancouver to Toronto over four nights and three and perhaps four days, is as close to the Wild West as you ever expect to get in twenty-first century railroading. It is an adventure every time, and you never know what will happen next. I, of all people, should know not to ride this train when I have anything of importance happening the day of arrival, or even the day after arrival. Yet here I am anyway, engaged in a great race I appear to be losing, badly.

I had planned to ride train 2 with a friend. The friend couldn't make it, and after I was ticketed, friends of ours in Washington, DC, said they would host an engagement party for our son Patrick and his fiancé, Kelly, this Saturday evening. My wife said to go ahead and ride the train. "If you make it, you make it," Cathie philosophized, "and if you don't..."

My plane out of Toronto leaves at 4:30 p.m. Saturday. If train 2 arrives as much as five hours late, at 2:30 p.m., I should still be able to make the flight. But I also instituted Plan B, which was to buy a cheap ticket on Air Canada from Sudbury, Ontario, to Toronto, leaving midmorning Saturday. If train 2 is eight hours late getting to nearby Capreol, I can bail out there and reach Toronto well in time for the 4:30 flight. And if train 2 is more than eight hours late? I'm screwed. And as of right now, with our train being serviced in Saskatoon, Saskatchewan, more than five hours late and still a day and a half from Capreol and two days from Toronto, it appears I'm screwed.

You're probably thinking my wife has already exonerated me. Yes, but I didn't like the look in her eyes the last time she said, "If you make it, you make it." And I don't want to disappoint my son and future daughter-in-law by standing them up. So now I am considering Plan C.

Let me bring you up to date. It has been a fun trip, as they all are on this train. I've made a bunch of new friends, including one man who knows all my Frailey relatives in Florida. The temperature has been below zero Fahrenheit from the moment I woke up the first morning in Kamloops, British Columbia, but on the train we've been snug. And believe it or not, we left Edmonton, Alberta, at midnight last night, on time.

Overnight, everything fell apart. By 6:15 this morning, we'd gotten only to Wainwright, Alberta, 125 miles. Do the math; that's an average of just 20 mph. Now it's 2:45 p.m., as we leave Saskatoon, and we've advanced only another 200 miles, averaging about 30 mph. The reason, of course, is freight train interference. The woods are full of 'em. Our assistant engineer was in the observation car to direct the backup move into Saskatoon. "I've never seen Canadian National this busy," he said. "We'll meet 15 trains in the next six or seven hours."

What is Plan C? To bail out in Winnipeg and fly to Washington from there. We're due there at 8:30 tonight, but I'm figuring 3:30 to 4:30 a.m. There's a noon flight to Reagan National that gets me to the engagement party a day ahead of time! Dear Old Dad will get extra credit for that.

Only a miracle will keep me on the *Canadian* past Winnipeg. A miracle means getting there in the wee hours no later than we now are and perhaps even sooner. But now it's snowing, there are those 15 trains to get past before we're even halfway to Winnipeg, and it's therefore hard to believe in miracles. I'll let you know how this works out.

Do you usually wake up on a train not when it is moving and knocking you about but when it is stopped? That was the case again this morning. It was 7:15 and starting to get light, and we were somewhere in Ontario. It seemed we'd been stopped quite a while, too. Wherever we were, I figured we were in the time slot of train 111, Canadian National's most important Do Not Disturb intermodal train. I had time to shower and dress and begin walking toward the observation car before the train whizzed past. Our engineer radioed best wishes to train 111 (I was right), and we continued on our way.

So, yes, a miracle did occur. I'm still on the *Canadian*. I did not get off in Winnipeg as I predicted I would. After Saskatoon, we flew along for a couple of hours, made up a little time, and I reconsidered my options.

As I said, the magic number is 8. We are due into Capreol, Ontario, at 12:18 a.m. tomorrow. If we can reach Capreol no more than eight hours late, I can easily catch the 9:55 a.m. Air Canada flight to Toronto, board my plane to Washington that afternoon, and arrive at Patrick Frailey's engagement party at about the time the *Canadian* limps into Toronto. That is Plan B, and I decided last night to go with it. Besides, I adore the lakes and forests of the Canadian Shield, and the forecast today was for snow. Who can resist all that?

I'm told we left Winnipeg at 4:05 a.m. this morning, 6 hours and 5 minutes late. As the day passed, we chipped away at the deficit, passing Allanwater Bridge at 1:00 o'clock this afternoon, now 5 hours and 29 minutes down. I began to relax. This might work.

Then the train dispatcher began sticking it to us. Just past Allanwater, we went in at Kawa to meet intermodal train 107. You need to understand that train 107 is a run-it-when-you-need-it train of no particular importance. But the *Canadian* is of even less rank, with the status of perhaps a work train that picks up old ties and scrap metal along the right-of-way. We waited 45 minutes for 107—long enough for me to walk to the dining car, have a bison burger, pay for my wine, and walk back to my room before it appeared. Three stations later, at Collins, we stopped 10 minutes to load two passengers waiting in a heated shed at the settlement. And at the next siding, Pascopee, back into the hole we went, this time for intermodal train 105. That was 50 minutes ago, and we're still waiting. In a couple of hours, it will be time to clear the decks again for another edition of 111, which is usually followed by train 101, another Do Not Disturb train bound for the docks at Vancouver, British Columbia.

OK, 105 passed as I wrote the last sentence. Our next stop is Armstrong, 15 miles away. We'll get there, spend 5 minutes and leave about 5:05 p.m., by then roughly 7 hours and 20 minutes late. My needle is about to enter the red zone.

I have two hopes. One is that a kinder, gentler train dispatcher is by now starting his or her shift in Toronto. The other is that the *Canadian* will be true to its reputation and, having gotten by 111 and 101 a few hours hence, will make up a slug of time. We'll know soon enough.

Several of you have emailed and messaged me to ask how things went. Did I make it to my son's engagement party Saturday night? To them I said yes, everything worked out. But while I did not tell a lie, I did not tell the whole truth. What follows is the whole truth.

As it turned out, train 2 was 8 hours late out of Hornepayne, Ontario, but made up an hour overnight. It rolled to a stop at Capreol, Ontario, seven hours late. The agent there said I'd have better luck getting a taxi to the airport from nearby Sudbury Junction and called one to meet me there. I got back on the train.

I was in Toronto by 11:00 yesterday morning. By noon I had checked in, gone through security and US Immigration and relaxed. Four hours later, the Air Canada agent is ready to board the plane to Washington. "Please have out your boarding pass and passport," he says. I look for my passport and it's not there. Gone. Vanished. Vamoose. Though I had already cleared immigration, the agent won't board me. I feel I had let down my family.

Where was the passport? I went to Air Canada's customer service desk and explained what happened. A woman took me by the arm, and we walked upstairs to US Immigration. "Stay here," she said, and disappeared behind a door. Thirty seconds later she emerged and beckoned me to follow her. An immigration agent handed me my passport, which I'd apparently dropped or left behind at the security checkpoint. The only thing he said was, "Mr. Frailey, is there any country you haven't visited?"

Back at the customer service counter, Air Canada put me on the next plane to Washington. I got to the party 2.5 hours late and embarrassed, but I was there. I think those 15 minutes of panic extracted a year from my life. There's no moral to this story, except stuff happens, and we have to keep our heads and roll with it. I thought I had prepared for every contingency I could, but a moment's inattention renders all the preparation in the world meaningless.

February 9, 10, and 11, 2017 Trains.com

TWENTY FIVE

THE TRAIN TO CORDOBA

"WHEN I WAS A GIRL growing up far south of Buenos Aires," said the concierge at our hotel in Argentina's capital, "the trains were so beautiful and fancy. To ride them was an event. Today? Eh! They are nothing." I had asked her about the passenger train from Buenos Aires to Cordoba, 440 miles to the northwest. "There is no train to Cordoba," she insisted with utter certainty. An hour later, I returned to our hotel to show her my sleeping car ticket to Cordoba. Being gracious, the concierge said only, "Please tell me about the experience when you return."

She was wrong in a narrow sense. There *is* a train to Cordoba. But she was really right. More than 30 years ago, on his trip down the Americas that produced *The Old Patagonian Express*, Paul Theroux sat for hours in the dining car of *La Estrella del Norte (North Star)* taking him from Tucuman to Buenos Aires, working on a four-course dinner that cost $2, served by "waiters and stewards . . . dressed more formally than the people eating." Later, in the heart of Patagonia, deep in Argentina's interior, he would complain of the cold, ceaseless wind that blew dust through the crevices of his sleeping car. But his description of the little narrow-gauge, steam-powered train that pulled wooden coaches the final miles to the end of the line in Esquel, literally the *Old Patagonian Express*, is of the stuff that has inspired wanderlust in otherwise sane men and women ever since. I happily accompanied my wife to Argentina as the corporate husband, for the chance to ride that country's trains. I was seduced by the anticipation of adventure.

Alas, long-distance passenger trains in Argentina have a poor reputation today, one that they appear to richly deserve. Those trains Paul
Theroux rode were products of the state-owned railway, Ferrocarriles
Argentinos, created when railroads were nationalized in 1948, during
the Juan Peron era. In 1993, the railroads were privatized again, and
that included the passenger trains. They have not fared well.

Most run only once or twice a week. Equipment is old and sometimes ill maintained. Schedule keeping can be iffy. Search on YouTube
for *El Gran Capitan* clips, and you will be entertained. But the reality is
different. *El Gran Capitan* runs weekly from the capital to Posadas, almost 700 miles north on the border of Paraguay, and the *Thomas Cook
Overseas Timetable* says about it: "This service is reported as running
up to 12 hours late on a regular basis. You are advised to take your own
water, food, toilet paper, etc." Daniel Thomas, editor and publisher of
Latin Rails, calls this train simply "an adventure." It may or may not
carry the advertised sleeping and dining cars.

You can ride *El Bahiense* six days a week south from Buenos Aires to
Bahia Blanca, about 425 miles, but the last time he did, the journalist
Thomas found dirty sheets in his room, atrocious food, and inattentive
servers. And you can venture into Patagonia from Bahia Blanca only
one day a week and only if the line is not closed by dust storms, as it
was earlier in 2010. At that end of the line, the *Old Patagonian Express*
still exists, but you must charter it.

The day before we left for Argentina, poring over the Cook timetable once again and making internet searches, I came upon my solution: that train to Cordoba, *Rayo de Sul*. Cook shows it with sleeper
and diner. Independently, Daniel Thomas emailed me to suggest it
and another train operated by Ferrocentral, the same *La Estrella del
Norte* that brought Theroux from Tucuman those many years ago.
I was unable to get a room to Tucuman the day I could travel, but there
was a room for me to Cordoba, meals included, for 300 pesos, or $75.

Had I visited Estacion Constitucion before riding *Rayo de Sul*, I
might have been forewarned. At that station, I later saw the sorriest intercity passenger train of my entire life being towed back for servicing,
four un-air-conditioned bench-back coaches and a diner, all adorned
by broken and shattered windows and all dirty beyond belief.

On the other hand, at first glance the train to Cordoba looked inviting under the lights of Estacion Retiro. But as I got closer, I saw something covering every window of the train: sheets of Lexan (a clear, rock-hard plastic-like substance). Penn Central used Lexan in lieu of glass windows on its commuter cars in the late 1960s to protect its passengers from stoning. But Lexan fogs over time. Plus, washing and other scratches add to the cumulative loss of vision.

What Ferrocentral had done was attach Lexan sheets about three inches outside of each glass window. There are mean-looking slums beside the tracks in Buenos Aires, but very soon into my trip the real cause became evident when I heard frequent swishing sounds outside. Trees and brush had been allowed to grow up to the tracks and gave passing trains a whacking.

The owner of the concession for these railway lines used by Ferrocentral, the freight train operator Nuevo Central Argentino SA, apparently feels the growth doesn't impede its freight trains and is unwilling to clear the obstructions. As its tenant, Ferrocentral either will not or cannot pay to clear the foliage for its twice-weekly trains. So its solution was to put this obnoxious Lexan over the windows of its dozens of passenger cars and call it a day.

I'd know in the morning how bad bad was. But now it was 9:00 o'clock, and I was hungry for a steak and some Malbec, Argentina's red wine of choice. Sitting down, I waited for a menu that never came. The attendant brought me and everyone else on the car a crepe-like appetizer filled with spinach and shortly thereafter the only main course, a shepherd pie, which is ground beef sandwiched between layers of mashed potatoes. It was filling, but I could feel depression coming on.

Daylight confirmed my worst fears. The Lexan shield over my window was doing its job well, deflecting batterings from the ends of tree branches. But the material was fogged beyond belief, and the scratches caused by limbs further impeded visibility. It was like looking at the world from inside a thick balloon or vision sometime after the onset of blindness. When we slowly passed a freight train waiting for us near Villa Maria, I could not accurately count the number of cars because it was impossible to see where one freight car ended and the next began.

OK, so I didn't enjoy *Rayo de Sul*. But I did sleep well enough and read a book the next morning as we trundled toward Cordoba. And besides, hadn't the concierge forewarned me? On the day I left Buenos Aires, I gave her a substantial tip. She invited me to return, and I hope I do.

October 29, 2010 TrainsMag.com

TWENTY SIX

YOU GOTTA LOVE THE SOO LINE

CAN YOU IMAGINE A MORE forlorn, out-of-the-way, and hard-to-reach railroad town in the continental United States than Portal, North Dakota? At the tippy-top of western North Dakota, right on the international frontier but not close to anywhere you'd ever need to go and shown on maps in type so small that you're not sure the place really exists... That's Portal. As a kid, leafing through the *Official Guide* in my room while I was supposed to be asleep, I'd come upon Portal in the Soo Line Railroad listing and wonder what it was like. An employee timetable circa 1960 showed one freight train a day making it to the Canadian border and back.

Although it took the greater part of a lifetime, I've finally made it to Portal. But far more interesting to me turns out to be those 550 miles spent getting there alongside this railroad, going generally northwest from Minneapolis to the Canadian border. I've come to regard it as North America's forgotten transcontinental railroad. Canadian Pacific, which now owns Soo, does in fact operate daily intermodal trains between Chicago and Vancouver, British Columbia.

This is a property that seems frozen in time. "We're just a sort of plodding railroad," one of its people told the *Trains* writer William D. Middleton in 1958, and the same could be said today, even though the pace has picked up considerably. In place of one freight each way a day, there are now seven or eight going to and from the corporate parent at Portal. (Soo Line Corp. still exists as a holding company, but the railroad is operated under the Canadian Pacific banner.) Vern Graham,

The nicest thing about tiny Portal, North Dakota, was its modern water tower.
Not so nice were the border guards, unconvinced I was merely chasing trains.
Fred W. Frailey

president of the Dakota, Minnesota & Eastern Railroad, a CP subsidiary, contends that the 430 miles from Glenwood, Minnesota, to Portal is the busiest single-track corridor in the United States dispatched by track warrant control.

The significance of that statement quickly becomes evident as I drive along the railroad for the better part of two days. Track warrant control dispatching means giving trains verbal instructions on meeting each other. Here's what is involved in meeting trains west of Glenwood, where the Soo is devoid of signals, power-thrown switches, and spring (self-relining) switches: The train taking the siding stops for the conductor to line the switch for the siding. The conductor of the train holding the main track stops to reline that switch for the main line. At the siding's other end, the conductor of the train in the siding lines the switch to reenter the main track. And the dispatcher tells the next train passing the location to stop and reline the exit switch. Each step takes longer than you imagine.

I am struck by another phenomenon: country grain elevators are alive and well at every little hamlet the railroad passes. I'm there during the harvest, and all the setout tracks are packed with covered hoppers waiting to be filled or picked up. These are not unit trains, unless CP is aggregating them into unit trains at its yards in Harvey and Enderlin, North Dakota. Rather, it's loose-car grain railroading on a scale I thought had ceased to exist decades ago. And every through freight I see except intermodal jobs 198 and 199 has setouts and pickups to make across each of the four subdivisions from the Twin Cities to the border.

So while this is a flat railroad, by and large, it is not a fast railroad. The intermodal runs will take 28–30 hours from the Twin Cities to Portal, and other trains most of two complete days or even longer. Case in point: At 5:30 p.m., I watch an eastbound train enter the siding in Eagle, North Dakota, population zero. The dispatcher says the opposing train will show up "in 10 minutes." But 90 minutes later, as night falls, my train still waits, and 14 hours after that I catch up as it prepares to leave Glenwood, just 153 miles down the pike. Or this: At Nashua, Minnesota, I pass an eastbound grain train that's easily 7,000 feet long, being pulled by a single GE locomotive. Half an hour later, the train still 40 miles shy of Glenwood, its conductor radios the dispatcher: "We're doing 15 mph and our time's up in two hours." The train ties down at Hoffman, Minnesota, having made a bit more than 100 miles in 12 hours.

Ah, Portal. There's not much to say about this little village, population 131. I see what appears to be a combined dance hall and motel and a gasoline station but no railway station. Employees of US Customs and Border Protection and its Canadian equivalent must be bored out of their minds because they seize on my arrival each way as they would that of an outlaw named Osama bin Laden. I am held for questioning and searches half an hour in each direction. Coming back to the United States, I see a Soo freight train get clearance faster than I do. Next time, I'll tell the border guards anything but the truth, which is that I am just watching trains. Once let loose, my fascination with Portal no longer exists.

But you've gotta love the Soo Line. I sure do. It's a low-cost, low-profile railroad that proved durable while railroads all around it failed or were eaten by competitors. "A little jewel" is what CP's chief executive called it in 1979, when the Milwaukee Road was two years into its final bankruptcy, the Rock Island was months from liquidating altogether, and the Chicago & North Western was kept alive mostly by Union Pacific's charitable interchange.

January 2011 Trains

TWENTY SEVEN

—ᴍ—

NEW YORK CITY, THEN

NO ONE SEEMS TO KNOW why they call it the Commission Hour, that period from 4:00 to 6:00 p.m. each Monday to Friday. Why not Confusion Hour? In 40 Office, the New York Division's dispatching center just off the Seventh Avenue entrance to Pennsylvania Station, it's a normal, rather unremarkable evening—bedlam, in other words. People shout across the room. Phones ring constantly. Voices of block operators boom over desk speakers of two dispatchers. Clerks, station workers, division officers move in and out like lemmings.

Amid all this, at A Desk, presides Edward DeBasky. Possessing the cocky assurance of someone who's been doing what he does for 29 years, Eddie DeBasky is totally in his element. "I'm 65 and could have retired two years ago. But I love it—just love it. In fact, my job gets more interesting the more that things go wrong."

His territory starts at Shell Tower in New Rochelle north of New York City, where Amtrak trains from Boston leave Metropolitan Transportation Authority rails, and extends over Hell Gate Bridge, past Sunnyside Yard, beneath the East River, through Penn Station, under the Hudson River, across the Jersey Meadows, through Newark, and west to Union Tower in Rahway. These are 40 of the most crowded, hectic, fast-paced, nerve-wracking miles of railroad to be found on earth. Block operators don't even try to report passing times to DeBasky as trains go by. They save up whole bunches of them—there just not time to do it any other way during the Commission Hour.

From A Tower in Penn Station: "121 with [motor] 900, 4:00 p.m. with 7 [cars]; 3721, 4:05 with 6; 3209, 4:10 with 6; 87 with 970, 4:15 with 14. Going east, 94 at 3:58 . . ." No sooner does DeBasky enter the figures on this six-foot-deep train sheet than Hunter Tower reports six by and Hudson ten by.

"At this time of day, everything is predetermined," he says during a quiet moment,

> and 90 percent of the time it all goes by the plan. Other times of the day, I can cross trains to another track to avoid a speed restriction, but not during the Commission Hour. Experienced tower operators I trust implicitly to handle trains. For instance, there are certain trains during the rush that regularly go from Track 3 to Track 4 at Elmora [Elizabeth, New Jersey], and Elmora knows to line the route. If a tower has problems, he'll let me know. Otherwise, they have too much to do, and I have too much to do, for us to constantly clear every move with each other.

Now it's 5:00 p.m., and westbound trains depart Penn Station at 3-minute intervals. A work trains wants to leave Hudson (almost two miles east of Newark), caboose in front, for Trenton; DeBasky moves it to Dock (just east of Newark's Penn Station) to await its next chance to move. The MTA dispatcher telephones to say that No. 175 from Boston will be at least 20 minutes late reaching Shell Tower in New Rochelle; DeBasky passes word to a clerk, who alerts Passenger Services. No. 87, the *Silver Meteor*, loses power three times because of low coolant levels on its E60 locomotive; it's 9 minutes late passing Union. The night chief dispatcher wants to be told if No. 152 gets a false indication at a home signal near Hell Gate—he's worried there's a problem the maintainers haven't fixed. Union asks if DeBasky will allow eastbound Conrail freight PIML to use Track 0 as far as Linden; the answer is no, at least for now. The B Desk dispatcher, who controls Union Tower to just west of Trenton, yells across that No. 184's air compressor quit and stopped the train at New Brunswick; it's reset 10 minutes later. New Jersey Transit's No. 5315, bound for Perth Amboy, reports an "undesired brake application" to the operator at Lane. "I want full particulars," demands DeBasky of Lane, once 5315 is again underway. "Have the engineer call me when he goes off duty."

The phone rings. DeBasky scribbles on a piece of paper, hangs up, and dials another number as three block operators seek his attention on the dispatcher's phone. "Commissary, this is the dispatcher. No. 175 needs some bar supplies when it gets here. Ready? Forty-eight bags of chips, 24 bags of nachos, 24 peanuts—what? How the hell do I know why he only wants 24 peanuts? And 48 beers. Got all that? No, I don't know what brand of beer. Now, go get 'em, tiger."

Portal Tower, at the Hackensack River drawbridge, is almost yelling for attention now. No. 184 lost its air again, this time on the critical two-track segment between Newark and Penn Station. Had it been a westbound train, there would have been trouble aplenty. "Let me know when he gets his air back," DeBasky instructs Portal. Two minutes later, Portal reports: "Eddie, 184 is moving at 5:46." "I could kiss you," DeBasky replies, "but I won't."

DeBasky is spared directing the densest flow of trains, over the 3.7 miles between Penn Station and Harold Tower, beside Sunnyside Yard in Queens. In the normal course of events, the train director at A Tower in the station controls this segment, which is just as well, because in prime times, Long Island movements occur on two-minute headways on Tracks 3 and 4, with Amtrak and NJ Transit equipment using Tracks 1 and 2.

By 6:30, the Commission Hour is past. The work train is by Union and in the hands of B Desk, Conrail's PIML gets its chance on Track 0, a minor crisis at Lane over a home signal at Lane that wouldn't clear is resolved, and 40 Office is becoming as . . . well, as quiet as it ever is at this time of day. You're exhausted. DeBasky asks you to return "when something really happens."

Over a railroad two, four, and six tracks wide, full of trains with different priorities and starting points and destinations and stops to make and speeds to observe, does DeBasky ever lose track of what trains are where when trouble occurs and he has maybe 10 seconds to decide the instructions to give to towers to unscramble a mess and keep his territory fluid? It takes longer to ask the question than for him to answer. "Hell no! I've been here too long for that. If I didn't know my trains by now, I'd be a damn poor dispatcher, now wouldn't I?" He's got you there.

You should have been in 40 Office at A Desk the next day, after all, for it was even more frenetic. A set of unattended NJ Transit MUs got loose in Penn Station and slammed cars on Track 1, and lightning from a summer thunderstorm knocked out signals between Bergen and Portal at the conclusion of the rush. Both events created havoc. Eddie DeBasky must have been in his element.

March 1985 Trains

TWENTY EIGHT

NEW YORK CITY, NOW

EACH WEEKDAY, 700,000 COMMUTER-TRAIN RIDERS and 35,000 Amtrak passengers aboard some 2,000 trains, in all, use some portion of the 457 miles between Boston and Washington, and the amazing thing is, it all gets sorted out. You see this most vividly in New York City. At the west end of Pennsylvania Station on weekdays, 479 trains arrive and depart, 347 of them belonging to NJ Transit and the other 132 to Amtrak. All but the 26 Albany trains traverse the two main tracks beneath the Hudson River. It's even more chaotic on the east end of Penn Station, where Amtrak's New England trains, plus Amtrak and NJ Transit deadhead moves to and from Sunnyside Yard in Queens, and finally trains of the Long Island Rail Road (LIRR)—in all, 796 trains—converge on four tracks under the East River. (Despite its 30-track storage yard on Manhattan's West Side, LIRR still dead-heads 56 trains back to Long Island each morning and brings them back that afternoon for reloading.) To accommodate this traffic, Penn Station has but 21 tracks, assigned as follows (track numbers run south to north): NJ Transit, Tracks 1–16; Amtrak Northeast Corridor, Tracks 5–16; Amtrak Empire Service, Tracks 5–9; and LIRR, Tracks 13–21.

Making all this work are people, some of them quite memorable. The voice of Penn Station the past 16 years has been that of Sheila Herriott, who announces from a small room off the concourse level. As you enter her cubicle, she's on the air: "This will be the final call, 7 West, for Amtrak 86, the all-reserved *Regional* service en route to Boston, departing 12:30. All aboard! For Stamford, New Haven, New

London" and so on down the list of stops. She never sounds excited or stressed but instead pronounces each word in an upbeat tone, crisply and plainly projecting an aura of cheerful authority. When you tell her this, Sheila just laughs. "You should be here," she says, "when all the trains are late, the phone is ringing off the hook, everyone wants to reach me, and meanwhile I'm making announcements. I'm not so professional at such times."

For many years, this job belonged to Danny Simmons, an excitable fellow who made his announcements from a different location high above the waiting room. Simmons, who could shout "All aboard!" and make it last five seconds, became such an institution he once appeared on the David Letterman show. (Search his name on YouTube.)

Penn Station also works because of people like red cap supervisor Maurice Robinson. "I've met two US presidents and many celebrities," he says. "I've talked to Hillary Clinton just as casually as we're talking now." You ask about tips. "Little old ladies tip the most," he replies. "They don't want to get caught in the stampede. But red cap service is free, and about a third of the people don't tip. That's fine."

Amtrak modernized its Northeast Corridor dispatching starting in the 1980s. But not so long ago ultimate authority over the entire, 40-mile New York metroplex, from Shell Tower in New Rochelle to Union Tower in Rahway, New Jersey, resided in a single dispatcher, who worked the A Desk from 40 Office, located off the waiting room, the tools of his trade a pen and a paper train sheet. Front line control was in the hands of 14 towers (four of them inside Penn Station) whose operators passed trains along, one to another. Only when things went wrong, which was often enough, did the dispatcher step in and issue instructions.

That's all changed. Of the 14 towers, only Dock, in Newark, is staffed today. In 1994, 40 Office became Penn Station Central Control (PSCC) and moved to a building off Ninth Avenue. During days and evenings, six Amtrak and Long Island Railroad employees control train movements in Penn Station and for several miles to the east (control point Gate) and west (Bergen). Five other dispatchers at PSCC handle Bergen (at the west end of the Hudson River tubes) to 20 miles east of Trenton, the start of the Mid-Atlantic Division.

The railroad near the Big Apple is out of capacity during the morning and evening rushes. The spoiler is those 10.1 miles from New York to Newark. This segment, with just two tracks, became crowded with the 1996 opening of the Kearny Connection at Swift interlocking, 3 miles east of Newark, to permit NJ Transit trains from former Lackawanna Railroad commuter lines serving Dover and Gladstone, New Jersey, to reach Penn Station. Montclair Branch trains followed in 2002. And in the middle of all this is Portal, a 104-year-old swing bridge over the Hackensack River whose openings halt trains and occasionally fail to close properly.

Amtrak's Gateway Program is intended to add capacity between New York and Newark, and is breathtaking in both its scope and projected cost. Envisioned are a new two-track Hudson River tunnel south of the present tubs, two more main tracks from the tunnel to Newark that will fly over the Hackensack, and a second two-track fixed span to allow the Portal bridge to be replaced. If the Northeast Corridor is to grow much beyond its present size, all of this is necessary. But the cost is $10 billion, most of it for tunneling, and only a pittance of that is funded. (Lack of money to accomplish these things remains an issue in 2020.)

However, hope springs eternal, so follow Amtrak's Clavel Crump, program director for engineering, fire, and life safety, to Tenth Avenue in Manhattan. From Tenth to Twelfth Avenue, and from Twenty-Ninth to Thirty-Fourth Street, work has begun on Hudson Yards, a multiuse development bigger than any other in the city, even Rockefeller Center. This whole expanse, including Long Island's West Side Yard, will soon be covered by skyscrapers. To preserve its ability to build that new tunnel, Amtrak is constructing an 800-foot concrete encasement—a box—to someday contain its tracks. Once it is in place below ground, up will go the 16 Hudson Yards skyscrapers. Still, that's not a tunnel, only the start of one, financed by Hurricane Sandy relief money. "Come back in six months," says Crump, grinning. "You won't believe the change. We'll have dug forty feet deeper."

April 2014 Trains

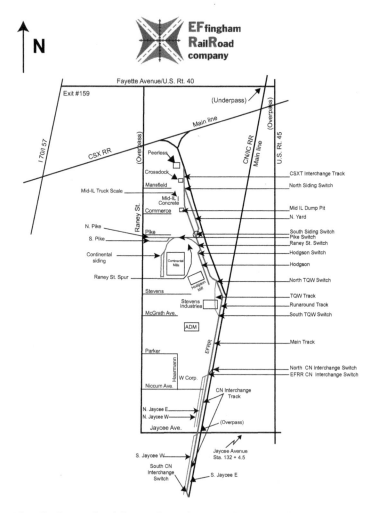

The Effingham Railroad, from end to end. Its main line is not as long as those of its Class 1 connections but just as wide. *Effingham Railroad*

—᚜—

TWENTY NINE

BEST LITTLE RAILROAD IN
EFFINGHAM

MAYBE IT'S THE MODEL RAILROADER inside me, but I'm discovering that really small railroads can be really cool. Even one that began life 15 years ago as a 400-foot spur.

That would be the Effingham Railroad. I'd never heard of it. Driving across central Illinois with Indiana Rail Road's Tom Hoback, I ask Tom the name of the owner of the Vandalia Railroad, another Illinois short line. "Charlie Barenfanger," he replies. "Charlie also owns the Effingham Railroad," Tom adds, opening his cell phone. "Would you like to talk to him?" Half an hour later we're sipping sodas with Charlie at the McDonald's in Vandalia.

Actually, Charlie no longer runs the Vandalia; Pioneer Railcorp owns it now. But he used that experience to start a new railroad from scratch in the nearby town of Effingham. North-south and east-west interstate highways and Class 1 railroads, the latter being Canadian National (ex–Illinois Central) and CSX (ex-Conrail), bisect this county seat of 12,000.

Charlie's strategic partner, Agracel Inc., an industrial development company run by Jack Schultz, bought a big chunk of land in the southwest quadrant of the CN-CSX crossing and erected a 200,000-square-foot warehouse. Other businesses followed. To serve them Charlie created the Effingham Railroad, beginning with that 400-foot spur off Conrail. The line has grown to almost 2 miles in length. Charlie is president, and Jack is vice president.

Charlie has a meeting he can't postpone but invites us to find the Total Quality Warehouse when we get to Effingham and ask for Luke. "He'll show you around," Charlie says, bidding us good-bye. He doesn't have to invite me twice.

At the warehouse, we meet Luke Perkins, 24, one of two full-time Effingham Railroad employees, having hired on after high school. His boss, Josh Storck, 34, superintendent of operations, is on vacation this week, making the Effingham literally a one-man railroad.

Luke leads us through the warehouse until an SW1200 becomes visible on an inside track. It still bears its Conrail number, 2716, and looks gorgeous in a paint scheme reminiscent of a 1955 Chicago Great Western switcher. "Want to take it for a spin?" Luke asks us.

Once we're aboard, Luke dons his throttle pack and brings the beast to life. Like a puppy, the 2716 trots out of the warehouse and trundles south to the CN interchange track, where I get off to take a photo. Then we reverse course, traverse the warehouse, and emerge on what I decide to call the Effingham Railroad's Northern Division, headed toward the CSX interchange.

At present, Charlie had said, the Effingham has three customers, which account for more than 2,000 carloads a year: the warehouse, a breakfast-cereal company, and a cement company. But a bakery occupying a former Krispy Kreme building is about to begin taking carloads, and the railroad offers rail-car storage. It's obvious, from the spick-and-span condition of the Effingham's infrastructure, that this is a successful business.

I ask Luke whether he and Josh really do everything. Yes, sir, he replies. Change cross ties and perform other track work? Yes. Maintain the 2716? Yes. In fact, when we leave, Luke plans to give his locomotive a wash "because it's got oil on it everywhere." Funny, I hadn't noticed; I guess I'm too used to Class 1 locomotives.

We come upon a second locomotive, beautifully painted (by Luke and Josh, naturally). On its flanks, the GP10 bears the name Illinois Western. Charlie had mentioned at McDonald's that he is starting this railroad 50 miles southwest of Effingham in Greenville, Illinois, using the same business model as the Effingham Railroad. According to Illinois Western's website, Agracel bought 700 acres next to CSX, and the railroad will build 3.5 miles to connect to BNSF Railway's Beardstown Sub, providing competitive rail access.

Tom and I need to get moving, so we thank Luke and reluctantly get back in my Dodge. I begin reflecting on the adventure that began two hours ago. What an interesting railroad. I begin running through my mind how I'd execute switching moves. Too late, I wish I'd asked Luke what it feels like to run a railroad all by himself. See, this tiny speck on the corpus of the railroad colossus is already firing my imagination. Railroading is more than just busy main lines and 70-mph intermodal trains.

October 2011 Trains

Burned out in two places and covered with the dirt of a new levee, Texas-Pacifico's bridge from Presidio, Texas, to Mexico is a useless relic in 2014—end of the line for the last big railroad-building project in Texas. *Fred W. Frailey*

—w—

LAST TRAIN TO TEXAS

LATE THIS AFTERNOON, PHOTOGRAPHER BOB Eisthen and I stand on a dirt levee in the Texas border town of Presidio. To our south sits Presidio's larger sister town of Ojinaga in Mexico. To our north, literally beneath our feet, a pair of rails is smothered by the recently built levee, and a few hundred feet farther north a timber railroad bridge lies buckled and destroyed by a fire. This is the end, in the United States, of Arthur Stilwell's dream to build a railroad with the shortest distance between Kansas City and the Pacific Ocean, the Kansas City, Mexico & Orient (KCM&O). A gap of a quarter mile separates the US and Mexican portions of his railroad, and through that gap trickles the Rio Grande, under the watchful eyes of Border Patrol agents.

Before you dry a tear, I should tell you there is a happy ending to this tale. Begun early in the twentieth century and the last big railroad-building project across Texas, the bankrupt KCM&O was sold to the Santa Fe Railway in 1928. An oil boom south of San Angelo allowed the bankruptcy trustee to dress up the pig and find a buyer before the boom busted. Santa Fe finished the railroad from Alpine, Texas, to Presidio and practiced benign neglect for many decades. Then about 1990, as it shed branch lines, Santa Fe abandoned most of the former KCM&O trackage in Kansas, Oklahoma, and north Texas and sold the lower 384 miles to a startup called the South Orient Railroad. The South Orient went belly up within a decade and sought to abandon the entire line. The state of Texas stepped in, bought it for practically nothing, and in 2001 or thereabouts awarded a 50-year lease to Texas-Pacifico Transportation, a subsidiary of Grupo Mexico, the Mexican mining conglomerate. Think of this as the regional railroad nobody ever heard of in the part of Texas where nobody ever goes.

At the time, someone said it would be a cold day in hell when Texas-Pacifico (TP) made money with this pathetic loser. Actually, I think that someone was me. The track was almost impassible, very few customers remained, and all were near San Angelo on the north end. Sure enough, TP regularly lost about $1.5 million a year. Had Texas not invested millions in shoring up the physical condition of this property, Texas-Pacifico would perhaps, like the South Orient, have given up. But Grupo Mexico, the parent of Texas-Pacifico, has deep pockets and hung in there.

Cut to the quick: It is today a cold day in hell. Hydraulic fracturing started south of San Angelo, in precisely the locale of the oil boom of the 1920s, and it is happy days all over again. Oilfield traffic, mostly fracking sand from the Midwest, is flooding onto Texas-Pacifico by the trainload. The railroad that had 8 employees at the start of 2012 now has 60. In 2012 and 2013, TP made back all its losses of the previous decade and has reinvested all of those newfound profits in the property.

So that's the story Bob and I have been reporting. Yesterday, however, we bid our good-bye to the busy San Angelo end of the railroad and headed south. By late afternoon we reach Fort Stockton, Texas, 161 miles down the road and as far as Texas-Pacifico has operated trains the past seven years. One reason is that there are no customers in the 147 miles beyond Fort Stockton to Presidio. The other is a burned-down bridge on the US side of the border; it stands in the way of international traffic.

We speak to the engineer and conductor of the Fort Stockton turn. They have just gotten back from Titan, 14 miles to the northeast, where they switched a fracking sand customer and exchanged cars with a turn from San Angelo. They can't switch their sand customers in Fort Stockton because a sand truck has bottomed out trying to cross the lead track and nobody has figured out how to budge it. We leave and an hour later call it a day in Alpine, Texas, 63 miles toward Presidio.

Today Bob and I decide to make it to the end of the line, to the burned Rio Grande bridge in Presidio. There will be no trains, of course, but we can't report a story on Arthur Stilwell's dream and skip Presidio.

Our trip is simply unbelievable. To begin with, the Orient—excuse me, Texas-Pacifico—uses trackage rights on Union Pacific's Sunset Route to get from Alpine across Paisano Pass, 11 miles. At Paisano, the rusty rails (70- and 90-pound product rolled before 1930) head south into what is, for lack of a better expression, utter loneliness. Near the Big Bend of the Rio Grande, the land is hilly and even mountainous, desert dry, and depopulated. God help you out here if your car gets in trouble.

US Highway 67 to Presidio runs miles and miles to the west of the railroad. We detour onto Ranch Road 169 for 25 miles, and just where the pavement gives out to a rutted path, we encounter our railroad. There is nothing in a 30-mile radius but a dirt-poor ranch house every now and then. But where Ranch Road 169 intersects the Orient is a place with a name in the current employee timetable (Plata), a siding (still), and a state historical marker. Never mind that nothing has gone over these rails the past seven years heavier than a hi-rail vehicle. We are fascinated.

The historical marker says that Plata once stood on the trail between San Antonio and Chihuahua in northern Mexico. It was settled about 1870 by John Davis of North Carolina, who established a peach orchard and trading post and would offer visitors peach brandy when they passed through on their way west or south. Others came, including Robert Ellison, who shipped 3,000 of his father's cattle by train to Alpine and then herded them south overland to Plata. It appears there were a lot of dry-land farmers who scratched out a living. Over time, all these farmers failed. Today the home of John Davis is in ruins, over which some sympathetic soul built a shelter to slow the inevitable decay. Bob turns to me and asks: "Who in his right mind would start a settlement here?" I have no answer.

When Santa Fe pushed the rails from Alpine to Presidio, it followed Alamito Creek for many, many miles. Of course, to call it a creek is a joke for 360 days of the year, but on the ranch road to Plata there are numerous depressions that are flooded in the rare rainstorms. Bob and I turn back to US Highway 67 and resume our trip to Presidio. Once there, Apple Maps shows us a way to reach the bridge, or rather, where the bridge once stood. But the streets Apple Maps says are there are not there. So I switch to Google Maps. Voila! You learn that in Presidio, streets near the international border are unpaved, unmarked by signs, and almost undrivable.

But we finally reach the levee that parallels the river. Bob and I are thinking: Are we allowed here? We've seen no signs to say otherwise. But 100 feet away from us is the river and Mexico. Sure enough, a green-striped Border Patrol vehicle heads toward the levee to intercept us. The agent, very friendly, asks where we're going. We tell him, and he says just to continue and we'll reach the railroad. This we do. Two fires, in 2008 and 2009, destroyed the US end of the rail connection in Presidio between Mexico and the United States. Texas-Pacifico wants to rebuild its part of the bridge; the Mexico portion, made of cement, still stands. If the bridge is ever rebuilt, we shall see whether this gateway is a viable connection between the two countries.

And we will see how long this oil boom lasts. It's a given that all oil booms end in busts (sometimes followed by new booms). Federico Diaz, the executive vice president of Texas-Pacifico, says to give him five years. In that time frame, his hope is to make the entire railroad operational, develop a diversified customer base, and be able to survive as a far smaller operation than today but a bigger one than before the boom.

All these thoughts swirl through my mind as Bob and I stand on that levee in Presidio. Before we leave, I take out my iPhone and click a photo looking north. Here the railroad remains a ruin. Of course, a few short years ago the entire railroad was a ruin, unable to make ends meet, even on a shoestring budget. But now, as I said, it is a cold day in hell.

(Note: Five years have passed since I wrote this. Only in 2019 did work start on a new bridge. Plans were afoot to restart train service between Fort Stockton and Presidio in 2020. Meanwhile, Texas-Pacifico remains busy servicing the oil drillers, so it's still a cold day in hell.)

February 22, 2014 TrainsMag.com

—m—

RAILROADING IN A FIERY FURNACE

ABOUT 4:00 O'CLOCK TUESDAY AFTERNOON, Tom Hoback and I drove across the Colorado River from Topock, Arizona, and entered California a few miles south of Needles. I glanced at the temperature readout on our rental car. It said 134 degrees. That day's *Los Angeles Times* had reported that the highest recorded temperature anywhere, ever, was in California's own Death Valley, in 1917. Then it was 136 degrees. That's how close we came to becoming living history. When I'd step outside, my exposed skin felt like it was being sandblasted. I could stand it about one minute. The wonder is that the tires on our car didn't melt.

I'll tell you something else that was smokin' in the Southwest this week. It was BNSF Railway. We followed the railroad Sunday from Cajon to Needles, California, on to Winslow, Arizona, on Monday, back to Needles on Tuesday and back to Cajon on Wednesday. Every day but Tuesday, wherever we were, was chockablock trains. The projected train count Wednesday (not a peak day) between Barstow and Needles was 85. That's as busy as the railroad had been in 2004, before the Great Recession, and far above the average train count for postrecession 2009 (64) and 2012 (71).

You're entitled to ask what is going on. Aren't the railroads in 2017 only starting to recover from what amounts to an industrial-goods recession that began in 2015 and lasted a full year? Isn't intermodal volume stalled out, or at least pretending to be? Isn't rival Union

Pacific the giant of the West? The answer to all these questions is yes. But . . .

The adjacent ports of Los Angeles and Long Beach may be the most unfriendly locales on the face of this earth to the transportation modes. But gosh, the volumes remain staggering, and BNSF appears to be walking away with the lion's share of the boat business. In reporting its intermodal loadings, the railroad declines to break out international from domestic business, one reason being that so much of what comes into Southern California in 40-foot ocean containers gets broken up at nearby warehouses and repacked in 53-foot domestic boxes that then get put on trains. So do you count that as domestic or international business? Nevertheless, Union Pacific does report domestic and international intermodal business separately, and in the last decade it has lost about one-third of its international volume. Based on what we saw in the Southwest, most or all of that migrated to BNSF—one "boat train" after another slithered across the desert.

And based on my casual observation, BNSF may have walked away with some of Union Pacific's finished automobile traffic. We saw a lot of auto rack trains and auto rack cuts of general freight trains that I wasn't used to seeing in years past, and one hears rumors as well.

Matt Rose, the executive chairman of BNSF, told an investment conference the other week that his railroad is not poaching Union Pacific's business. Yeah, sure. But something sure as hell is happening to cause those trains to appear at streetcar frequency. In last year's slump, BNSF carried 5 percent fewer loads, but UP, 7 percent fewer. So far this year, BNSF's business is up 6 percent from a year ago; UP's, half as much. Draw your own conclusion.

I'll also leave you with the story of our journey across the Needles Subdivision from its namesake town to Barstow on Wednesday. Engineering had the south track out of service at midmorning between Ash Hill and Ludlow. (Ash Hill is where the tracks separate, leading to all those gorgeous photos of trains spread all over the desert landscape.) Westbounds shot out of Needles at about 20-minute intervals, and eastbounds from Barstow at least as frequently. The eastbounds included the priority trains, except for a train of empty ethanol tanks that led the pack.

A timetable page of the middle of the Needles Sub would look like this (the north track being Main 1 and the south track Main 2):

	Milepost	Notes
EAST AMBOY	660.0	Crossover 2 to 1 (9,359-foot siding on 1)
WEST AMBOY	661.8	Crossover 1 to 2
BAGDAD	669.3	
EAST SIBERIA	674.8	Crossover 1 to 2
WEST SIBERIA	676.6	Crossover 2 to 1
EAST ASH HILL	686.3	Crossover 2 to 1 (8,066-foot siding on 1)
WEST ASH HILL	688.2	Crossover 1 to 2
LUDLOW	693.4	Double crossover

So as Tom and I watched this unfold on my ATSF Monitor software (which reveals train locations and the lineups of signals and switches), the plan the dispatcher put in place was this: Stack up the westbounds on Main 1 at East Ash Hill (the start of single track that morning) and points east until the parade of eastbounds got by. But leave Main 1 open between East Siberia and West Amboy for Z-LACWSP8 (Los Angeles–Willow Springs, Illinois), the hottest thing on wheels that morning (think UPS, UPS, UPS, and more UPS), to zap around the empty ethanol train, which was halted at West Amboy.

Then . . . wouldn't you know, just as the pressure of opposing trains built to a climax and the plan started to unfold, Z-LACWSP8 tripped a hotbox detector 212 axles back. At 10:00 o'clock, it came to a halt right at the East Siberia crossover, and the conductor, Jose Ortega, alighted. Fort Worth was asking every five minutes for updates. Let me just say Mr. Ortega got some transportation assistance and was at axle 212 in no time. But it took him 30 minutes to inspect axle temps, hand brake positions, brake rigging on the offending car, and those on each side for several car lengths and then recheck them to conclude that nothing was wrong. Remember, if he certified the train as safe and it derailed a mile later, Mr. Ortega would be looking for another line of work. Meanwhile, the eastbounds stacked up on Main 2 behind Z-LACWSP8 like Chevys at a stoplight. And of course, westbounds could not get on the single track until the eastbounds cleared. The ethanol train in front of Z-LACWSP8 got a signal and went on its way, unpassed.

One train after another got on the radio to say it had two or three or four hours of time left to work, and only one patch (relief) crew had been called at Barstow. "If you ran us like a Z train, we'd make Needles," one conductor said, to which the dispatcher replied, "If I could run you like a Z train, I wouldn't be sweating so much right now."

At 10:45 a.m., the conductor, Ortega, was back on his General Electric horse. Eventually the train began to crawl forward. But for the longest time nothing else moved. That's how a jackpot behaves; nothing happens quickly. Tom and I could get out of the car (it was only 107 by then on Wednesday) and see seven or eight or nine or ten trains at once, depending upon how we interpreted the distant lines of equipment on the sweeping curves. Realistically it would be midafternoon before the mess was dissolved. And as we got off of Historic US 66 and onto Interstate 40 at Ludlow, here came the next alpha dog, Z-LACWSP9 (again, think UPS, UPS, UPS, and more UPS), out of Hobart Yard in LA 90 minutes behind its unfortunate brother, the 8 section. Somehow it would have to pass all those trains in front of it. I cannot imagine how.

You can interpret what I've just told you two ways. One is OMG, what a screwed-up railroad. I interpret it as the sweet smell of success. Stuff happens. You deal with it. The train crews and the dispatcher and Mr. Ortega and those who got him to axle 212 and back to the GE locomotives all worked it out. BNSF Railway these days is a mighty machine. It creaks and squeals at the pressure points, like Ash Hill, but it works.

June 22, 2017 TrainsMag.com

THIRTY TWO

NIGHT TRAIN TO NOWHERE

MIDNIGHT IN STAUNTON, VIRGINIA, ON a summer weeknight so quiet you can almost hear your pores sweat in the humidity. On the edge of downtown, a truck door slams in C&O Flats. That would be Steve Nicely, the engineer on tonight's train Z631. It will operate over what had once been the original Chesapeake & Ohio main line but is now the Richmond & Alleghany Division of the Buckingham Branch Railroad.

Perhaps some explanation is in order. Go back to 1987. Annie Bryant enjoys her walks after returning home from teaching school in suburban Baltimore. Then one day her husband asks to join her. This is new, Annie thinks. What's bugging Bob? Soon it tumbles out. Bob Bryant, just retired and of modest means, wants to buy a railroad. Annie is momentarily floored. Bob has always talked about owning his own business. But a railroad? Now he's serious, and he wants her to be part of it.

Against all odds, they do buy a railroad. Today the 17-mile, broken-down short line (the Buckingham Branch) that Bob and Annie purchased with a personal loan from their village banker in Dillwyn, Virginia, has become a 275-mile network. It hosts unit trains, Amtrak's *Cardinal*, and uses centralized traffic control over 125 critical miles. Welcome to "Mayberry RFD" in real life.

So here you are in Staunton, to ride Buckingham Branch's night train. Waiting for Nicely is the operations manager, Zane Craig, subbing for the regular conductor. Tonight's job: Take two light engines, a

The summer sun is just appearing over the horizon as Buckingham Branch train Z631 climbs Knob Mountain near Goshen, Virginia, at the end of a long night. *Fred W. Frailey*

GP40 and GP40-3 still in Kansas City Southern colors, 56 miles west to the big CSX yard in Clifton Forge, Virginia. Pick up whatever CSX has for them and head back east, perhaps setting out cars at a tie-treatment plant in Goshen, Virginia. Back in Staunton, deliver cars to the short line Durbin & Greenbrier Valley (D&GV); then tie up and go home. They collect their paperwork and start the two diesels. By 1:00 a.m., they're on the main line, making 40 mph.

Bob (a former CSX marketing manager) and Annie paid $45,000 for the original Buckingham Branch, which served his boyhood home at Dillwyn. They had but two other employees. But they made a go of it, and in 2004 their railroad successfully bid to lease CSX's scenic, mountainous line from Richmond, Virginia, to Clifton Forge via Charlottesville, 190 miles. CSX has another, water-level route between those two cities, but it was too congested to handle all the traffic. What makes the lease work for Buckingham Branch is that CSX guarantees to route at least four empty westbound unit trains a day over the leased line, providing trackage rights revenue.

At 2:32 a.m., Steve Nicely brings Z631 to a halt at JD Cabin, the western end of Buckingham Branch trackage, on the outskirts of Clifton Forge. Zane Craig radios the CSX yardmaster: "Coming off the North Mountain Sub with two light engines for the Forge." Replies the yardmaster: "I've got your cars. Q302 is leaving. Then I'll try to get you in." Half an hour later Z631 comes to a stop on Track 3.

Craig drops off to see what's there. He finds 40 freight cars in all, 19 for Staunton or points east and the other 21 for the tie plant. But they had noticed going by it earlier that the tie plant is plugged with freight cars, so these will have to wait for another trip.

They assemble their train and then repeatedly try to rouse the yardmaster for a signal out of the yard. No reply. Couldn't Steve just walk over to the yard office, 100 yards away? "He isn't there," Steve says. "The yardmaster is in Huntington, West Virginia, and covers every terminal on the Huntington Division." Oh, the wonders of Class 1 railroading!

But the yardmaster does respond when a CSX coal train on the fuel pad says it's ready to go to Richmond on the water-level route, and he tells Z631 to follow that train back to JD Cabin, where it will return to home rails. Zane Craig relays this information to the Buckingham Branch dispatcher, whose little office is near where this crew went on duty tonight in Staunton. Their dispatcher informs them that several trackage-rights trains are coming against Z631. It's almost 5:00 a.m. as their train leaves Clifton Forge. This will indeed be a long night.

They're scarcely out of town before the dispatcher radios: "There's a westbound CSX train coming to Staunton. How far east do you want to go for it?" After some discussion, he says he'll line Z631 into the siding at Goshen to meet one and maybe two trains. "The second train is short and moving fast."

Catching two westbound trackage-rights trains on the eastbound leg of Z631's run is not uncommon. Steve and Zane wait at Goshen 15 minutes for the first to go by with coal empties and another 45 minutes for the second, with empty grain hoppers. Leaving Goshen at 6:50 a.m., their train slugs up a 1.5 percent grade at a steady, monotonous 18 mph. Talk in the locomotive comes around to railroad life.

Zane: "You've got to have a passion for this work. If you don't love it, you'll go crazy."

Steve: "A friend asked why I don't work for CSX. I grew up in Clifton Forge and still live there. I said I don't want to work for that railroad. We're a close-knit family on the BB. If you have an issue, you can walk right up to the boss and talk about it. At CSX, you probably will never see the person you work for."

Asked whether jobs are assigned by seniority, the two men just laugh. Employees decide among themselves who works which jobs. And if there's no train, there's always something else to do, even if it's clearing brush.

The talk helps you all keep awake as the sun rises. Steve and Zane have Z631 back in Staunton a few minutes after 8:00 a.m. Leaving eight cars on the main track, they bring the front part of their train down an incline to interchange with the Durbin & Greenbrier Valley. That railroad's GP7, with a father-and-son crew (dad doing the ground work), is waiting. Steve pushes the cars onto a pickup track. The D&GV crew retrieves them and leaves.

Then Steve and Zane back their light engines onto the main line, recouple, and push the train into their vest-pocket yard at C&O Flats. As they kill the engines, a third westbound CSX trackage-rights train whistles its way through town. The first Buckingham Branch train of August 11, 2011, marks off duty at 9:00 a.m.

January 2012 Trains

PART III

KICKING THE TRAIN
DOWN THE TRACKS

THESE ARE STORIES THAT DON'T fit neatly into the sections of the book about railroad management or my travels. Yet they are reflective of my writing about trains and the people who work around them, and they include some of my best-told tales. For instance, one of the more obscure railroad stories I ever wrote was about "income certificates" issued by the Missouri-Kansas-Texas Railroad in 1958, to prevent its bankruptcy. But in rereading how C. Glenn Cameron thwarted two attempts by Union Pacific to purchase the Katy decades later by buying up these certificates and holding out for a higher price, I realized what a wonderful financial story I had written that had nothing whatsoever to do with locomotives or passenger trains or Form 19 train orders. So I included it in this book. Bravo C. Glenn Cameron! Read it and marvel at this man's nerve.

I've been wrong before. When Congress in 2008 mandated positive train control (PTC), a technology that should prevent most collisions and overspeeds, I was skeptical, arguing that railroads were being required to spend billions to save relatively few lives. That remains the case, but I've had a change of heart. The quicker PTC can be made operable (the latest and possibly last deadline is the end of 2020), the sooner the public will have confidence in the safety of railroad operations, and maybe the sooner we can put engineerless trains on the tracks. "Moments I'd Rather Forget" is about three other times I screwed up. All three occasions are funny in the telling, and enough time has passed that I can confess my sins.

Imagine NIMBYism on a regional level. Such has been the case in Florida for several years. A new company, first called All Aboard Florida (but then branded Brightline and now called Virgin Trains), is ramping up a for-profit passenger-train system between Miami and Orlando. Trouble is, its trains won't stop for the 200 or so miles from West Palm Beach to Orlando, which has the locals in the "exclusion zone" up in arms. Towns have spent literally millions, to no avail, opposing this service that doesn't serve them. When a well-known novelist who writes about idiotic Floridians joined the NIMBY crowd, his hysteria made him look like a wacko character in one of his own books. Read all about it in "What's the Matter with Florida?"

One summer day in 2012, thinking up things to write about, I remembered a Northeast Corridor drawbridge over the Bush River north of Baltimore that Amtrak opens twice a day on weekends. But it's not your typical drawbridge. Workers must literally disassemble the track to permit the bridge to be raised. I decided I'd like to see this occur and arranged with a yacht club near the bridge to take me there on a Sunday morning. I'd spoil the ending of "A Little Drawbridge That Couldn't" if I told you what happened. I'll just say that all hell broke loose.

The phone rings. It's Cliff Black, Amtrak's press liaison, asking that I write about the chronic lateness of the *Auto Train* at the hands of the host railroad, CSX. In fact, I was about to do just that, except that Cliff didn't know. So I held out, saying (correctly) that to best describe the train's woes between northern Virginia and central Florida, I needed to make the overnight run aboard its locomotives—both ways. To my surprise, Cliff instantly agreed. "Saturday Night Fever" came about because, on the way back from Florida, things didn't go as expected.

Stan Kistler is one of the iconic legends of the railfan world, a guy whose photographs I grew up seeing in *Trains*. Along with people like Richard Steinheimer and Donald Sims, Stan helped brand the magazine after World War II for standout railroad photography. Imagine my delight to be able to spend two days in his company on BNSF's Clovis Subdivision ("The Ageless World of Stan Kistler"). Driving through Abo Canyon—with permission, I should add—in our rented car, we shredded a tire and returned to Albuquerque to swap vehicles. The next day, on right-of-way roads we encountered a burgled container train stopped by thieves. There is never a dull moment around this gentleman. And everyone Stan encounters, including me, he charms.

I include one story from my way-back-when. It's 1955, and I am all of age 11, a budding railroad enthusiast who cannot get enough of trains. What should occur one morning but a head-on collision of two Kansas City Southern freights a mere three miles from my front door. For the better part of a week I am beside myself, cycling from school to collision site, barely able to contain my excitement. Decades later, reporting my first story for *Trains*, I talk to the chief train dispatcher of KCS in Shreveport, Louisiana. I mention to him this collision, and he reaches into a file drawer and gives me his complete file on that long-ago calamity, including the actual train orders that were issued. "The Wreck of Old 54" is an account of that fateful event—and an object lesson to anyone who thinks rules alone can prevent tragic mistakes.

My friend Tom Hoback worked for Harry Bruce in marketing at both Western Pacific and Illinois Central railroads, and they remained friends. When Tom lent me Harry's privately published memoir, I was stunned by what he had accomplished at IC. As Illinois Central's president, he trimmed the failing railroad to a profitable core by selling groups of branch lines and, in so doing, spawned a slew of regional railroads, most of them successful over time as well. "The Man Who *Really* Saved Illinois Central" is my tribute to this resourceful man. He is also, it turned out, elusive. For a month, I tried to track Harry down as he drove around the country; I never succeeded. The closest I got was a thank you letter from the man after the piece appeared—with no return address, of course.

I end this book with a humdinger. If you think railroads have problems today, consider "The Mother of All Traffic Jams," about the ultimate modern train mess. In a sentence, UP in 1997 tried to merge its trains with those of Southern Pacific, which it had bought a year earlier, before the two railroads were ready, and the result was bedlam. In its public explanations, UP insisted it had done nothing stupid, when in fact it had done a lot of stupid things. When I could no longer stomach the company line the railroad was dishing out, I started making phone calls even as UP employees were shoveling reams of internal memos my way. The result was this news analysis, which has stood the test of time wonderfully. Read it and be thankful we're not having one of these today. But we will, be assured. In railroading as in life, history repeats itself.

—⚏—

THIRTY THREE

MISS KATY'S FUNNY PIECES OF PAPER

SELDOM IF EVER HAS A Wall Street analyst derailed a merger. But Katy Industries didn't reckon on C. Glenn Cameron when it agreed to sell its Missouri-Kansas-Texas Railroad (MKT) to the Union Pacific subsidiary Missouri Pacific last May for $108 million. Katy paid dearly for its carelessness. A group of investors assembled by Cameron sidetracked the merger not once but twice and perhaps for good.

Who is C. Glenn Campbell? He turns out to be a 47-year-old analyst who follows rails for Moseley, Halgarten, Estabrook & Weeden, a small New York brokerage. "We wear lots of hats here," he says. "If you're good at selling, you sell your own recommendations. This isn't the typical research department."

To explain what he did requires backing up to 1958. That's when MKT was descending into a decade-long flirtation with bankruptcy. The property was falling to pieces; cash was nonexistent. Unpaid dividends on Katy's preferred stock totaled $166 a share, a $73 million obligation that threatened to topple the railroad. A complicated transaction ensued. Each share of preferred plus the dividend owed its holder was exchanged for, among other things, an "income certificate" with a face value of $110. These financial instruments were close to being unique: no interest, no voting rights, no maturity date—just an obligation by Katy to redeem them using a sinking fund created by future earnings. They also contained an early version of the merger-busting "poison pills" so popular today. Neither Katy nor a successor owner of the railroad could pay dividends to shareholders until 60 percent of the issue had been retired.

By 1985 Katy had fixed up its railroad, secured coal-hauling contracts to utilities in Oklahoma and Texas, and begun, in 1976, to make money, although never enough to activate the sinking fund. Two decades of trying to find a place for itself within a larger railroad finally bore fruit with the Union Pacific offer.

Reading the merger announcement on the Dow Jones ticker awakened Cameron's curiosity. "I hadn't thought about these certificates for 20 years," he says. "I wondered what had happened to those funny pieces of paper." It turned out they had been delisted by the American Stock Exchange in 1975. Everyone had forgotten about them. They were traded sort of by appointment only; most of them lined trunks in peoples' attics. But it wasn't lost on Cameron that with the certificates still in public hands, Missouri Pacific as Katy's new owner could not pass along profits (pay dividends) to the parent, Union Pacific. Cameron started calling clients, and they began buying the certificates in over-the-counter markets for as little as $17. When Katy Industries as a condition of the railroad's sale tendered for them at $25 payable upon consummation of the merger in 12 to 18 months, Cameron's group bid $27 payable in five working days. Before long Cameron & Company accumulated roughly half of the 667,005 certificates at an average price of about $24.

They had Katy Industries over a barrel. Of course, no certificates were returned to Katy by Cameron's people. The tender offer was a flop. In October 1985 UP terminated the merger agreement. When Katy Industries upped its bid to $33.50, UP reinstated the merger deal. Still no takers. On January 13, 1986, UP canceled the merger a second time. Just 18 percent of the certificates had been tendered.

Bear in mind that the Katy is in good times barely in the black (it earned $6 million in 1985 on revenue of about $260 million) and that no other buyers are making themselves known. Yet Cameron insists that a price approaching the $110 face value is possible. At its present rate of profitability Katy will begin retiring the certificates in six or seven years. Redemption Day would come sooner if it sells assets, the capital gains being treated as profits. Katy already has industrial property in

Dallas and San Antonio for sale. Then there is Katy's wholly owned, 589-mile subsidiary, the Oklahoma, Kansas & Texas (OK&T), a Fort Worth, Texas, to Salina, Kansas, grain feeder acquired from the bankrupt Rock Island in 1980. Cameron figures OK&T ought to be worth $100 million and suggests Burlington Northern as a possible buyer. He says he has talked to other parties interested in Katy, including people outside the Class 1 railroad business.

Union Pacific could return to the table yet again. Nobody disputes that Katy's main route from Kansas City to Dallas and Fort Worth and the stretch from Fort Worth to San Antonio are superior to those of UP-owned Missouri Pacific. "I'm willing to wait," insists the analyst. So it seems is Katy Industries. The chairman, Wallace Carroll, told the *Wall Street Journal* his company would "keep on running the railroad—it's a good property." If they prevail, Cameron and his clients will be among the few investors in the second half of the twentieth century to make money on Katy securities of any sort. But they may not prevail. The analyst Henry Livingston of Kidder, Peabody & Company notes that the income certificates stand last in line for MKT's net income and other available cash, behind a long line of other obligations. As for BN buying the OK&T, he says BN seems more intent on maximizing return from its existing rail lines than in buying new ones. Concludes Livingston regarding Cameron's position: "It doesn't look like a smart investment. Speculators end up being wrong once in a while—for getting too greedy."

All this leaves the future of the Katy tied up in a stare down between a group of investors with $8 million at stake on one side and its corporate owners on the other. In Katy country, this is called poker.

(Katy Industries and UP soon folded their cards and surrendered. In May 1986 Katy offered $39.75 per certificate, almost three times what some of Cameron's investors had paid, and a sufficient number were tendered. The Missouri-Kansas-Texas Railroad joined the Union Pacific family on August 12, 1988.)

April 1986 Trains

THIRTY FOUR

—∿—

MOMENTS I'D RATHER FORGET

HERSHEY, NEBRASKA, LIES TEN MILES west of Union Pacific's big North Platte yards. Every time I pass Hershey, as I did the other day, I leave US Highway 30, cross the tracks, and continue to Hershey Super Foods. There, I stop and peer respectfully at the little Dumpster behind the grocery store. Yes, the Dumpster. I'm convinced it was there, on May 10, 1995, that I threw away my notes for one of the most important stories I ever wrote for *Trains*. Unfortunately, I've had more than one humbling experience. Confession being good for the soul, I'm going to share a few of them with you.

"Super Railroad!" shouted the cover of the November 1995 issue, its feature section devoted entirely to the 285 miles of Union Pacific that lies between Council Bluffs, Iowa, and North Platte. The brainstorm of Kevin Keefe, the editor of that era, it involved a dozen writers and photographers. The cool thing about this package of stories: We explained this segment of Union Pacific (and by implication, all of contemporary railroading) through the prism of one day's journey of a lowly manifest freight train, CBNP (for Council Bluffs–North Platte). The date chosen for this group effort was May 10, the anniversary of the completion of the First Transcontinental Railroad. My part in all this was to ride the locomotive of CBNP and gather information that would be spread throughout the package of stories, including my own lead article, which Kevin cleverly titled "Colossus of Roads."

The trip across Nebraska goes exceedingly well. Needless to say, I enjoy myself thoroughly aboard CBNP, getting to know the engineer,

Dennis O'Connor, and the conductor, Phil Tamisiea. Also in the lead unit is John Bromley, head of public relations for UP and a prince of a fellow who would become my dear friend. By the time we stop in North Platte, it's 4:00 o'clock and my reporter's notebook is full of facts and quotes.

So what do people with names like Frailey, Ingles, Lustig, and McGonigal do after a day of riding and chasing trains? They chase more trains, is what. Honored to be with writers of their caliber, I pile in and off we go in two cars. The first stop is the Hershey grocery to get soft drinks and snacks. While we're at it, we clear the car of a day's worth of trash and throw it in the Dumpster. It's while we return from watching coal trains on the South Morrill Subdivision that I reach to my hip pocket for my notebook and discover it empty. Where's the notebook? We stop and search every inch of the car's interior. Nothing. Could it have fallen out at one of the places we got out to watch trains? Possibly, but there's little light left, and I'm convinced I threw it away in Hershey with the trash. So back we go to the grocery. I climb into the Dumpster. It's not there, or at least I cannot find it. All 285 miles back to Omaha the next day I sit in the back seat while David Lustig tells nonstop funny stories to Keefe, who is driving. But I'm in a total funk.

The end of the tale is this: I confess my boo-boo to Bromley, who rewards me with a two-inch-thick recitation of every passing time of every train at every control point during the hours of our trip. From that and slides I took of every train we met, I reconstruct events of that day. And I reinterview O'Connor and Tamisiea. Ultimately, the story gets written.

But it happened again! Several years later, Union Pacific invites me on a special train run for transportation reporters, between Los Angeles and Kansas City. CEO Dick Davidson is aboard and is his usual affable, interview-friendly self. I talk myself onto the locomotive at Tucumcari, New Mexico, and the engineer insists I run his train (with him hovering over my shoulder) for an hour or so. Then we are sidetracked to meet a freight train, and I disembark from the E unit, to walk back on the right-of-way to the body of the train and let someone else have the experience I just did. Soon I realize my notebook is missing (dare I say *again*?). Back I go to John Bromley, who has the track searched the next morning. A couple of days later, the notebook is delivered. Agreed, I should not stow notebooks in my rear pocket.

Now fast-forward to the spring of 2003. I'm writing a profile of Kansas City Southern and ask to see the line between Shreveport, Louisiana, and Meridian, Mississippi, now called the Meridian Speedway. The editor Mark Hemphill and I fly to Meridian and are met by Jerry Heavin, the VP of operations. A KCS business car is attached to the end of hotshot I-ATDA (Atlanta–Dallas) and off we go. After dinner that evening, served by two attendants, Jerry asks if we'd like to join him on the rear platform, and we wind through Vicksburg, Mississippi, and over the Mississippi River. The view is spectacular in early evening. Soon a light rain begins to fall. Time to go inside, we agree. But we cannot, because the door leading to the car's interior is locked—from the inside.

We bang and bang on the door, to no avail, because the attendants have gone to bed at the other end of the car. Jerry gets onto his stomach and tries to reach and turn the angle cock, which would apply brakes to the train. The valve is tantalizingly out of reach. When might we stop next, I ask Jerry. Shreveport, he replies, in about four hours. It's raining harder now, and we're all chilled.

Our only hope is that we'll meet a train and transmit our SOS by voice. After what seems an eternity but was probably only an hour, the wish is granted. We see the reflection of a headlight, from a train in a siding. At the sight of the conductor standing beside the locomotive, we scream in unison several times, "Stop this train!" A minute later, the brakes take hold. Once stopped, I walk forward along the tracks and begin throwing ballast at the compartment occupied by the attendants. Pretty soon a light comes on, the shade comes up, and they understand our predicament.

Some time or other, poor Jerry Heavin had to explain away the pane of glass I cobwebbed. I wonder what he said.

November 2016 Trains

THIRTY FIVE

THE TIMELESS CLOVIS SUB

OVER BACON, EGGS, AND WHOLE-WHEAT toast at Cooks Cafe, Allan Potter casually stirs his coffee and remarks, "We'll see 106 trains through here in the next 24 hours." Potter is describing railroad life in Clovis, New Mexico, where he's the terminal superintendent for BNSF Railway. The long and short of it is there never seems to be a letup astride BNSF's transcontinental line (better known as the Transcon) through Clovis. For instance, outside the cafe and across US Highway 60, a crew is boarding an eastbound vehicle train on one of the lead tracks. "Nine V trains came through yesterday," explains Potter, putting down his napkin. "Two weren't touched. The other seven we had to work. This train was created from cars those trains left behind."

As he gets up, Potter's Blackberry beeps. He looks and puts it away. "The Altbar just went into emergency at West Texico," he says, employing BNSF slang to refer to a manifest train marooned a few miles east of here. "That's the one you're riding, isn't it?"

By now you've learned this much: it's going to be an interesting day on the Clovis Sub.

If you know anything about the Clovis Subdivision, it's probably that the west end is anchored by Abo Canyon, the rugged and inaccessible gorge that takes the railroad over the tailbone of the Rocky Mountain range. But the canyon occupies fewer than 4 of the 239 miles between the terminal towns of Clovis and Belen. What's to be said of the other 235 miles across the eastern half of New Mexico? As it turns out, a lot.

A BNSF freight rushes past Cardenas, New Mexico, at 70 mph while 32 miles to the east the old hotel at Ricardo is all that's left of a once-flourishing community. *Fred W. Frailey*

It's here, halfway between Chicago and Los Angeles, where the Transcon comes together—literally in 1906, but figuratively as well. Imagine a nor'easter building almost to tornado force, heading west from Kansas. At Avard in northern Oklahoma, the fury is strengthened by trains from Tulsa, St. Louis, Memphis, and Birmingham. They're joined in Amarillo by traffic from north Texas and points southeast. Finally, at Texico on the Texas–New Mexico border, come the trains from Houston, Lafayette (Louisiana), and New Orleans. Now the train count averages close to 90 a day, peaking at more than 100 on heavy days. Clovis is where the full force of this storm first hits.

Anyone fascinated by how railroads are run will quickly be drawn to the Clovis Sub. A good place to start is where US 60 goes under the railroad just west of Fort Sumner, New Mexico. You're at CP (control point) 7197, the west end of a short stretch of single track that gets trains over the Pecos River. You'll see for miles in either direction. Now watch (and listen on frequency 160.590) as the dispatcher in Texas prioritizes the order with which trains get possession of that precious track—Railroad Operations 101. This and two other single-track segments make the Clovis Sub as difficult to manage as any other part of BNSF between Chicago and California.

Do you appreciate the West's history? Then come upon the ruins of downtown Vaughn or the ghost town of Yeso, where an upright piano waits in the long-abandoned community center for another Saturday night dance that will never come, and wonder: What dream brought people here—and what harsh reality drove them away?

This is big, lonely, windy country, and it can sneak up and inhabit the soul of the most taciturn train watcher.

In March 1907, the last piece of what would become today's mighty Transcon fell into place. Tracklayers working from both directions met at a barren desert spot they named Duoro, 19 miles east of the settlement of Vaughn. Not until December 18, 1907, would bridges, ballasting, and station construction be finished and service begin on what is known today as BNSF Railway's Clovis Subdivision.

The Santa Fe Railway had run trains into California since 1884 and to Chicago since 1888. But Santa Fe's first Transcon involved a tortuous

4 percent grade over Raton Pass on the Colorado–New Mexico border and, 157 miles farther to the southwest, a 3 percent grade through Glorieta Pass. Those grades hadn't mattered so much early on, because the flow of freight traffic to and from California had been just a trickle. As business began to grow in the first years of the new century, Santa Fe choked on those grades. In time, they would have doomed the railroad.

This was a fortuitous era for the Santa Fe, which had emerged from receivership in 1895 and resumed its expansion. It took full control of its line from Albuquerque to California, by buying out Southern Pacific at one end and St. Louis–San Francisco at the other. And it came under the wing of one of its great leaders, President Edward P. Ripley (1896–1920). By 1901, Santa Fe had assembled a spindly branch line extending more than 700 miles, from southern Kansas and a connection with the main line to Chicago. The branch meandered through the Texas Panhandle to Clovis and then south to Roswell, New Mexico, and ultimately Pecos, Texas. Ripley asked his chief engineer, James Dun, to investigate joining this line with the Santa Fe main line just west of Albuquerque. That's how it all began.

Early in 1902, Santa Fe's legendary locating engineer, Meredith Jones, was sent into the desert with his crews to find a way to get freights off the Raton and Glorieta Mountains. The route Jones surveyed was indeed superior. He held grades to 0.6 percent except for 21 miles of 1.25 percent eastward from the mouth of Abo (pronounced A-bow) Canyon to the summit at Mountainair.

Santa Fe then had to rebuild the skeletal Pecos line from Clovis all the way back to Kansas to handle mainline traffic. But it now possessed an asset, the best and ultimately the busiest route to California. So just a little foresight by Mr. Ripley, leveraged through the decades by successors named Gurley, Reed, Krebs, and Rose, paid undreamed-of dividends.

West of Fort Sumner, you take a moment to look at the countryside. Only one word does it justice: empty. Empty of people, and except for fencing, empty of any sign people ever lived either here or in almost any of the other former settlements across the 71 miles from Fort Sumner to Vaughn. Even cows are few and far between; it takes between

40 and 55 acres to sustain a single animal. Two miles down the track from today's Ricardo crossovers is the site of the former depot. In a 1912 photograph you find, it appears as a handsome, two-story stucco structure bordered by a flower garden. In 1910, 333 people lived in and around Ricardo.

North of the tracks, from your car on a right-of-way road, you see the ruins of Ricardo's eight-room hotel, the same one that 7-year-old Zorene Todd noticed the day, a century earlier, when her family arrived from East Texas to homestead. The town also had a post office then, plus a general store, barber shop, blacksmith shop, and four or five saloons. By 1940 the population of Ricardo had dwindled to 115, more than one-third of them children. In 1980, at age 79, Zorene Todd Thompson returned to see what she could of Ricardo—and needed the help of a rancher's son to locate even the cemetery, which had been part of her family's landholding. So completely has time erased this village that the only evidence it ever existed is that old hotel.

Lots of people came to eastern New Mexico to dry-farm the land, planting beans, corn, and root crops. But like Zorene Todd's father, they all failed. Today the depopulation of the Clovis Subdivision between Fort Sumner and Vaughn is all but complete. If anything, the landscape between Vaughn and the village of Willard, 40 miles west, is even more inhospitable than the depopulated land to the east. The difference is that nobody ever tried to farm west of Vaughn. In fact, the only viable communities left on the Clovis Sub are Fort Sumner (population 1,060) and Mountainair (1,078). Neither could be called more than mildly prosperous. Vaughn (population 469) has been laid to waste commercially, and Willard (253) has even fewer signs of community life. Those who stick it out in the ranching economy are poor, stubborn, or both.

So the contrast between a booming railroad bursting at its seams and the defeated communities and ghost towns—and that eight-room hotel in Ricardo waiting for the west wind to blow it over for all time—is startling. God giveth, and God taketh away, is one way to reconcile the contrasts. It's all here to see on the Clovis Subdivision, birthplace of the Transcon.

(Note: In the dozen years since this piece was written, the Clovis Sub has undergone much change. BNSF literally moved mountains to create a second main track through rugged, isolated Abo Canyon on the subdivision's west end. It also built, again at great expense, a second spectacular bridge to put two main tracks over the Pecos River in Fort Sumner, and closed a third single-track gap just west of Vaughn. But some things are unaltered. For instance, the hotel that is all that remains of Ricardo still stands by itself, near the railroad tracks in the desert, defying a west wind that never ceases.)

April 2007 Trains

THIRTY SIX

WHAT'S THE MATTER WITH FLORIDA?

CARL HIASSEN WRITES FUNNY NOVELS that catalogue and poke fun at the stupid things his fellow Floridians do—their petty crimes, feckless behavior, outrageous acts, crazy blowups, and on and on until you're rolling on the floor. But now in real life, Carl Hiassen is a character in what could be one of his own books.

It all has to do with All Aboard Florida. In 2012, when Florida East Coast Industries revealed its plan to run 18 unsubsidized passenger trains each way a day between Miami and Orlando, mostly over tracks of the affiliated Florida East Coast Railway, politicians could not have been more praiseworthy. Chief among the chanters of hosannas was Rick Scott, the Republican governor who in 2009 turned down the offer from the federal government to build Florida a high-speed railroad between Tampa and Orlando; he's taken a lot of heat for that stupid decision. *Everybody* loved All Aboard Florida.

It must be Florida's drinking water. I mean, there's a reason it's so easy for Carl Hiassen to write such hilarious novels about stupid people. Now it's two years later and it seems as if the state is rising up in righteous anger that Big Rail (as it's now known) is about to stuff its unsubsidized passenger trains down the throats of innocent people who never asked for those trains but who will now be subjected to their noise and vibration as they whiz past their oceanside villas at 79 to 125 mph. The politicians have turned against All Aboard Florida, as have some newspaper editorialists. And look, leading the charge, with a demented grin and a sharpened cleaver in hand, it's Carl Hiassen himself!

Yes, Carl Hiassen is also a columnist for the *Miami Herald,* and he put a measured dose of sarcasm into a recent column. "The whole project," he wrote, "is anchored on the dubious notion that millions of people can't wait to hop a train from Miami to the Orlando Airport (via Cocoa). Its web site sunnily predicts that three out of four passengers will be tourists. Tourists who are what . . . afraid to fly? Too scared to drive? Talk about a narrow market." He predicts AAF will be a colossal bomb and signs off with, "All aboard, suckers."

He's only one actor in this reality show. Governor Scott is now testy toward AAF, warning it in a letter not to expect a penny of state support. His opponent in this November's election, Republican-turned-Democrat Charlie Crist, said this to a newspaper: "This All Aboard Florida thing: I'm not going to denounce it, but I have serious concerns about the whole thing . . . It seems like a lot of people on the East Coast aren't real interested and aren't all aboard."

Crist refused to come down one way or the other, but with friends like this, who needs enemies? But oh, they are out there. Every munici-pality along the way seems to want mitigation, also known as gimmes. Gimme Number 1 is quiet zones, which they may get. Gimme Number 2 is free bandwidth on fiber-optic cable a FECI subsidiary is laying. Gimme Number 3 is to move FEC freight trains to CSX Transporta-tion either south of West Palm Beach or all the way to Jacksonville.

And people who drink too much of Florida's water are just going wild. Whole websites exist to stoke the fires of their anger. This from Karen: "They don't give a flying horse whose homes or lives are af-fected by their stupid train they need to take it and shove it." From Carolee: "We should be charging them to run through our area! How in the world did this thing get through?" From Blake: "What does this brand spanking new company know about railroads? What are their qualifications, credentials? Judging by the route they chose, it appears they know NOTHING other than how to pay off politicians." From Rodica: "Why we need Train America in the middle of very beautiful City? In the Middle of happy people?" For the most part, these are people along the Treasure Coast north of West Palm Beach. There will be no stops between West Palm and Orlando, so the residents of these communities get the crossing gates going down 36 more times a day but no discernable benefits.

I do feel their pain, but I call them stupid because they're worked up and risking a stroke over nothing. There is no way petitions, politicians, civic proclamations, or anything else can stop All Aboard Florida. The Surface Transportation Board says it's not an interstate business and not in its jurisdiction. AAF is seeking to finance $1.6 billion of the project's $3 billion cost through a low-interest government loan. An environmental impact study conducted as part of that loan process suggests minimal changes that I'm sure AAF will agree to. The loan program, Railroad Rehabilitation and Infrastructure Finance, was set up for just such projects as this; the only question is AAF's ability to repay. Without that loan, All Aboard Florida says it has lined up alternative financing.

AAF is the brainchild of Wes Edens, cofounder and chairman of Fortress Investment Group, which owns FEC Railway and FEC Industries. Fortress manages $64 billion of assets. If Edens is willing to bet $3 billion that his folks can make a go of All Aboard Florida, I'm willing to bet Carl Hiassen $100 that he will succeed.

But that's OK, Carl. You may owe me a Ben Franklin someday, but you have the plot line for a great comic novel now in hand.

(Note: All Aboard Florida, now known as Virgin Trains US, operates its passenger trains between Miami and West Palm Beach, and has begun building improvements that will extend its trains to Orlando. And last time I looked, Carl Hiassen was still writing columns bashing the enterprise.)

December 2014 Trains

—ᴧᴧ—

THE BRAIN DRAIN

WHEN I WAS DECADES YOUNGER, I regarded most people over the age of 60 as dangerously out of touch. They were not hip. As I have gotten older, my attitude has softened (surprise!). To use a newspaper metaphor, it's about legs. Young reporters have legs, which is to say, energy. They gain knowledge and experience from that energy, and as their legs wear out, they become wizened editors of a younger generation of reporters. They develop better brains, in other words.

Railroads today are in the midst of a brain drain. A great generational change is occurring, and railroads are unprepared. The legs remain, the youngsters, but fewer and fewer of the wizened people with the brains. Senior people are checking out, taking retirement and with it their knowledge of this complex business. The people replacing them all too often aren't yet up to the task. You see this at every level. A major terminal of a western railroad operates at less than pre–Great Recession levels, allegedly because its young managers lack moxie. A train dispatcher tells me that delays on his railroad increase because younger colleagues cannot execute complex strategies. And of how many up-and-comers in top operating jobs could this be said by a railroad executive: "He's a nice fellow, went to leadership school, and knows all the processes. But he's clueless whether his trains are on time."

All of this gets me to John Rebensdorf, a name you've probably never heard. John is symbolic of the generation of railroad managers calling it quits. He came to Union Pacific out of Harvard Business School

44 years ago, attracted by "The Godfather," legendary president John Kenefick. His first job was budget research in the accounting department. But in his spare time, when he wasn't riding freight trains to learn the railroad, Rebensdorf began doing operations planning, something altogether new at UP. In his book *Union Pacific: The Reconfiguration*, the historian Maury Klein says: "He looked at power assignments and found that shortages occurred because power was assigned without reason. A North Platte local, for example, got three high-horsepower units even though only one was needed for the tonnage hauled. The same pattern existed all over the system. Gradually Rebensdorf made himself the point man on cost and profitability analysis."

As years went by, his reputation and responsibilities grew. Rebensdorf's title in later years was vice president of network planning and operations. But to the extent UP had a strategic planner, it was John. Jim McClellan, one of the industry's great strategic thinkers, says someone once called him "Norfolk Southern's John Rebensdorf." Adds McClellan: "That was one of the nicest things anyone ever said to me." One coworker talks of John's "breathtakingly comprehensive knowledge" not just of Union Pacific but of its competitors and connections. "He coupled a genius-level IQ with deep passion for railroading and an insatiable quest for more information," says this person.

A whole generation of Union Pacific people trained under Rebensdorf, including Jim Young, once the company's chief executive, and Jack Koraleski, formerly the chief marketing officer and Young's successor. So did Dennis Duffy, who headed operations for Union Pacific for many years. Working for John was never easy. To quote Maury Klein: "Rebensdorf was considered an oddball. An intense, serious perfectionist, he demanded as much of others as he did of himself. He took pride in his work and could be difficult to deal with." Difficult? John's temper is legendary. When it is aimed at you, as once happened to me, you feel a foot tall.

I can't remember how I came to know Rebensdorf, except that it was a long time ago. But I'll never forget my first impression of the man, garnered from a telephone interview. Simply put, I was stunned by his candor and breadth of knowledge. You never heard BS from this man's mouth. His refusal to spin a serious problem by prevaricating is a

John Rebensdorf hallmark. For example, Rebensdorf's staff warned in 2002 and 2003 that a stunning manpower shortage was about to overwhelm the railroad, caused by a wave of retirements of engineers and conductors and a surge of new business. But the president, Ike Evans, anxious not to upset the upward thrust of earnings by taking on new employees, expressly rejected the warnings, says the historian Klein, and CEO Dick Davidson would not overrule Evans.

The result was what I called UP's "mini-meltdown" of 2004, a service crisis that cost the railroad hundreds of millions of dollars and tarnishes its reputation to this day. In its public pronouncements, UP said it was blindsided by the retirements. Not so, Rebensdorf told me at the time, refusing to toe the company line. As he said to Klein: "The decision not to hire additional crews came directly . . . from Ike Evans." That is vintage John Rebensdorf, telling it like it is and letting the chips fall.

Within Union Pacific, Rebensdorf maintained a somewhat private, even aloof, presence, although he remained always accessible. His desk was always clean. When you needed his knowledge, I am told, out it came, everything he knew, "delivered with appropriate irony," as one person puts it.

At the end of May, John hung it up after 51 years in the business. God help Union Pacific. Losing John is like cutting off your own fingers. Says a colleague: "I firmly believe he walked out of UP with knowledge of agreements or arrangements with other railroads that no one in the building knows about." While his former job was filled in name, I am told UP divided John's responsibilities among three people. If so, I'm surprised that is all it took.

October 2012 Trains

THIRTY EIGHT

A LITTLE DRAWBRIDGE
THAT COULDN'T

YOU KNOW WHEN YOU CROSS a drawbridge. There's a distinctive *klunk* when your train moves gingerly over that joint separating terra firma from the movable portion of the bridge and a second *klunk* as you reach the other side. But the Bush River bridge on Amtrak's Northeast Corridor? I had to be reminded a drawbridge still exists. Acela and Northeast Direct trains cross this half-mile-long concrete and steel structure, 24 miles north of Baltimore, in less than 15 seconds at unreduced speeds of 125 mph. Forget *klunk*; there isn't any.

That's because, for all but a few hours a week in summer, there is no drawbridge at Bush River. For the bridge to be raised, Amtrak workers literally disassemble fixed, bolted rails and move them aside. Then when the bridge is lowered, they reassemble the track structure into its previous semipermanent state. The Bush River bridge occupies a category all its own.

The Bush River is a broad, brackish body of water that empties into Chesapeake Bay. In the era of 80-mph top speeds, the Pennsylvania Railroad and Penn Central were content to man a conventional drawbridge when needed, and the Bush River was no impediment. But the development of a 125-mph track structure by Amtrak made continued use of conventional miter rails all but impossible and the bridge problematic. Denied by the Coast Guard from permanently closing the draw span in 1977, Amtrak instituted the present system of taking the bridge apart to make it movable. As stated in the Code of Federal

Regulations, from May 1 to early October, each weekend morning and afternoon, those special openings occur.

Curiosity got the better of me. One Saturday in June 2012, I call the Bush River Yacht Club, which deals with Amtrak on opening times, and find myself talking to Henry Bahr, the club's power fleet captain. Henry says to show up the next morning, and he'll have someone take me to the draw in a motorboat to witness the opening.

I'm there bright and early. Henry introduces me to Don Schlissler Sr., and in Don's boat we motor out to the bridge.

It's 8:00 o'clock. At the north end of the bridge we see a cluster of men in orange helmets gazing toward the club. If no boats appear, they can collect their overtime and go home. But one by one the boats do appear, and a dozen guys make the long, careful walk to the draw span. By 8:15 they're cranking up generators, emptying tool sheds on the bridge deck, and taking apart the first of the two tracks. The southbound *Palmetto* goes by at 8:30 on its way to Savannah, Georgia, and now the railroad is theirs. Catenary wires are deenergized. *Rat-tat-tat* go air-powered wrenches. A Speed Swing putters out to lift the detached rails out of the way with its boom.

At 8:45 the bridge motor whirs, gears engage, and the draw begins lifting. Very quickly, 13 boats pass beneath the span. Most belong to members of other Chesapeake Bay yacht clubs who had visited overnight. Five minutes after it opened, the draw is lowered.

Now two parallel realities occur. What I see with Don is a dozen well-trained people hunkering down to put back together what they have just taken apart. The Speed Swing places the rails in their approximate place. We hear sledgehammers nudging them into exact position and then the *rat-tat-tat* of bolts being tightened. At 9:20 the crane put-puts back to the north end of the bridge, and the crew begins to follow. All is at peace. We wait for the first train to pass. Hmm, that's odd—no trains. We finally give up and return to shore.

The other reality is utter calamity. When you work on the railroad, you don't have to make things up. It seems every imaginable, or unimaginable, weird scenario eventually happens, and one of those scenarios is happening now. What we can't see, because we're on the west (inland) side of the bridge, is the breakage of a pulley holding a cable that raises and lowers the catenary wires in line with the draw span. When the pulley snaps, down plunges a 1,600-pound counterweight tied to the other end of the cable. Now it's hanging over the river on one side of the bridge, overhead wires are out of alignment, and the Northeast Corridor is out of business. The men calmly walked away because until more help arrives, there's not a damn thing they can do.

While Don and I wonder why no trains appear, Amtrak's people swing into action. Supervisors in Philadelphia, Wilmington, Baltimore, and Washington round up diesel locomotives and qualified engineers to pull trains between Baltimore and Wilmington. (It never happens.) Charles Matlack, assistant division engineer, is rousted from home and sent to the bridge. Hours go by. Trains are canceled or combined. But mostly trains sit and wait.

Not until 1:27 p.m. is the Bush River bridge reopened. Matlack reports later that the challenge was getting the counterweight raised so the catenary wires could be returned to their correct positions. "We finally took the bucket off the Perryville catenary car and used its boom to push up the weight," he says. Some 30 Amtrak trains are delayed for periods ranging from 10 minutes to 4.5 hours, four others are terminated en route, and one is canceled. Goodness knows how many apologies are uttered by conductors over PA systems. It's a memorable day on the Northeast Corridor. And there I float, oblivious to the bedlam in the making.

September 2012 Trains

In Depew, New York, near downtown Buffalo, I finally see the former New York Central as it once was: four tracks wide. *Fred W. Frailey*

THIRTY NINE

THAT COMMODORE
VANDERBILT FEELING

COINCIDENCE? THE EVENING BEFORE I begin exploring the former New York Central across upstate New York, my wife and I taxi
past Grand Central Terminal in the rain. I see the bronzed and lighted
statue of the Dutchman himself, looking proud and (it seems to me)
a bit vain. What a combination of character traits he possessed: in-
telligence, cunning, stubbornness, resourcefulness, foresight. In his
82 years, Cornelius Vanderbilt (Commodore was a nickname) built a
maritime empire and then, with his son William, laid the foundation
for one of the greatest railroads the world will ever see.

My friend Mark Hinsdale and I drive across upstate New York to
see what remains of that Vanderbilt railroad. At its zenith in 1950, this
line, now owned by CSX Transportation, was four tracks wide, two
tracks on the south side for the 68 weekday passenger and mail trains
that toiled alongside the Mohawk River and two on the north for the
26 scheduled freights and whatever extras showed up. An army of lev-
ermen in 39 towers and other 24-hour offices between Albany and
Buffalo oversaw the operation, passing trains from one to another in
imitation of 19th-century English railways.

All this came crashing down soon thereafter, thanks to jet aircraft,
the New York State Thruway, and the decline of manufacturing in
the Northeast. In the late 1950s, Alfred E. Perlman tore this structure
apart, replacing directional running on four tracks with bidirectional
signaling on two tracks. The towers closed, as later did gothic passenger

stations in Albany, Syracuse, Rochester, and Buffalo. Perlman did the right thing and probably saved the company. But what is left to remind you of the Commodore's magnificent railroad?

Quite a lot, starting with the foundation his family laid. The Vanderbilts built across New York as if anticipating the high-speed trains of the 21st century. Their right-of-way is remarkably straight, deliberately missing many communities to achieve the desired alignment. And they elevated their tracks through towns, even small ones. Road crossings are few and far between. All of this remains a generous legacy to CSX.

Perlman kept the two passenger tracks, leaving half the right-of-way empty except where Track 3 remains in place as sidings. You notice this starkly beneath the signal bridges, which are now twice the needed width, or where twin, two-track steel bridges, one of them now empty, cross streams. Those signal bridges and their signals are easily of 1950 vintage. By year's end they will be replaced.

But Mark discovers that those passing tracks are really the pre-Perlman Track 3 rails, left in place lo these decades. In the Little Falls siding, for instance, I find 1947 date stamps on 127-pound rails, the standard weight adopted by Plimmon Dudley (1843–1924), who was New York Central's chief metallurgist. And here and there you'll find old towers, such as Signal Station 30, slowly disintegrating on Utica's east side, and Signal Station 15 in Lyons, now used as a crew room. Other traces of the past: the West Shore Railroad remnant used as a bypass around Rochester, foundations of the coaling towers and icing platforms at Wayneport, and the restored Beaux-Arts passenger station in Utica (now with but two tracks).

As for the trains, the variety is rich by 2012 standards. The count is just over 50 a day. Eight are Amtrak's. Roughly half of the CSX freights are intermodal runs, many of them calling at Dewitt Yard in Syracuse. Dewitt acts as a mixing bowl for intermodal traffic to and from Boston-Worcester and northern New Jersey, the latter handling double stacks and the former being all single level, owing to lower clearances. The rest is a mix of manifest, automobile, and unit grain, coal, and ethanol trains.

A couple are worth waiting for. Twice a week in each direction come the Railex vegetable trains run in partnership with Union Pacific from

California and Washington to the Railex warehouse in south Schenectady. Trains Q090 and Q091 are unmistakable: 60 or more white, 60-foot refrigerated cars, each one defaced by graffiti.

My prize catch is Q001, which zips past in the rain north of Port Byron with 47 United Parcel Service vans. This is the CSX portion of the "bullet train" inaugurated in 2003 with UP. UPS sought to match the four-business-day ground service between the New York City / Boston and Los Angeles areas that Federal Express had begun via highways. Weekends made this easy. Only the packages collected Mondays and dispatched early the next morning required super expedited schedules to be delivered Fridays. UP sustained its side of the bargain less than a year before these trains became victims (and partial causes) of its mini-meltdown of 2004. Today UPS drives its Tuesday trailers between Chicago and LA. But CSX still upholds its end. Q001 leaves Little Ferry, New Jersey, across from Manhattan, at 4:00 a.m. Tuesdays, combines with a Worcester section at Selkirk Yard near Albany, and passes Buffalo by early afternoon. Sister Q002 crosses New York on Thursday afternoons.

I've saved the best for last. At Amtrak's Depew station in east Buffalo, we come upon unadulterated, pre-Perlman New York Central. For almost two miles each way, there still exist the four tracks of once-upon-a-time, protected by those classic signal bridges. I look east. I look west. My imagination must supply a streamlined Hudson fronting the *Empire State Express*. But at this special place, I finally get that Commodore Vanderbilt feeling.

August 2012 Trains

FORTY

—ɯ—

THE AGELESS WORLD OF
STAN KISTLER

WHEN WELL-MEANING PEOPLE ASK WHY I like trains—or sometimes, why I *still* like trains—I usually think for a moment, feel all those conflicting emotions boomeranging around, and reply that I no longer know. I do know what drew me to trains as a kid: those big, loud locomotives; men doing honest work; rides on a caboose being shunted; listening to dispatchers practice their craft. It was love at first whistle. Those things still matter, but now I'm also fascinated by railroading as a business, the dollars and cents. So getting back to that question, it's complicated.

Not so for Stan Kistler. Stan is 82 years young. When I was just learning to walk, he was advertising his photographs for sale in *Trains*. When I struggled with my dad's Argus C3, he was taking the cover photo for the April 1958 issue of *Trains*.

"Why do I like trains?" Stan wrote to me recently. "It's who I am! Yes, that simple. It's been part of my life more than 70 years, and it is not going to change." I should adopt that reply myself.

To my mind, Stan is among the most fortunate of train lovers. As a kid, during the closing years of World War II and just afterward, he lived in San Diego and then Pasadena, California. Our nation was at the end of a tragic war from which we emerged stronger. President Ronald Reagan would later speak of "morning in America," but the late 1940s was a morning-in-America era, as well. Stan could bicycle safely from suburb to suburb or take the Pacific Electric cars, to reach the steam railroads. Smog in the Los Angeles basin seemed to come mainly from smudge pots in the orange groves. The great transition from steam to diesel power was in full flower. Southern Pacific, Santa Fe, and Union Pacific were all reequipping their streamliners and adding new ones. What a great time and place to be a kid watching trains.

And the people! Reading my first issues of *Trains* in the mid-1950s, I would scan the bylines of California articles and study the photo credits: Richard Steinheimer, Donald Sims, Donald Duke, Gerald Best, Henry Griffiths Jr., Walter Thrall, Chard Walker. And yes, Stan Kistler.

The 1982 book *Growing Up with Trains: A Southern California Album*, by Steinheimer and Sims, captures that era well. Most of those men, all giants in my formative years, are gone, but not Stan. Let me give you a taste of what the man is like.

He and I and our friend Tom Hoback are bouncing around in a minivan in autumn 2013 on a private road alongside BNSF Railway's Clovis Subdivision in New Mexico. When a track supervisor spots us, he stops and asks who we are. He explains that a double-stack train had just been stopped by a red flag placed between the rails, and several containers were broken into. In the time it just took me to write that last sentence, Stan and the supervisor are exchanging addresses and discussing BNSF people they both know. Soon we come upon that train, still stopped, and Stan and the conductor begin talking like lost buddies. And finally we see the special agent from Clovis, and Stan befriends him as well. They're both friends of former Santa Fe cops in California. Stan Kistler is like an infectious disease that makes you feel better.

Later we talk in the car. If he were a teenager today, I ask, would he be out here watching trains? Stan laughs. Of course! "I watch these young guys. They are all into scanners and digital things. That's fine, and I wish we had those things when I was their age. I had a switch key and once in a while could get into a phone booth in the boonies and listen to the dispatcher line to find out what was going on. That was fun, but also risky. Railroads are so depersonalized today. I got to know so many railroaders as a kid. In San Diego, when I was 13 and 14, they adopted me in the passenger yard. I was riding switch engines all over.

In Pasadena, the enginemen would get down to oil their engines and talk to you. I made a lot of good friends that way."

Stan describes a morning in San Diego with his grandfather. At 6:00 o'clock they walk to the Santa Fe yard and see a *San Diegan* being readied to run. "There was a guy in white overalls climbing around. We went over to talk to him. Would we like to see the inside of the engine room? Sure. He takes us inside an E1. He was tightening something down on every cylinder. Now shall we start it up? Young man, you go push that button over there. I got to start an E1. Pretty cool."

His first trip to Cajon Pass was August 15, 1945, as the United States was celebrating Japan's surrender in World War II. "I was 14. It was nothing like today. Half the trains would have FT diesels and half would be 2-10-2s. Helpers were anything they could come up with, including 2-8-0s. Route 66 was two lanes. There were no smog regulations. That was the Southern California I remember as a kid." You will find that world in *Stan Kistler's Santa Fe in Black & White*, as fine a book of Santa Fe photography as will ever be published. I remark that it must have seemed like heaven on earth. "I thought so!" Stan replies.

Stan stops and looks at me in the back seat. "Fred, this was fun. Can we just watch trains now?" And that's what we do.

April 2013 Trains

SATURDAY NIGHT FEVER

"WE'RE GOING TO GET SLAMMED tonight."

David King is an experienced and earnest Amtrak engineer, and when he looks me in the eye and says the *Auto Train* will be hogtied once again by CSX, who am I to argue? Precedent is on his side. For the past 49 days, not a single *Auto Train* has arrived in Lorton, Virginia, or Sanford, Florida, within 30 minutes of the appointed time, and two trips in each direction were canceled to recalibrate the train sets. I'm aboard the locomotive of the northbound *Auto Train* tonight to document the next shellacking.

King utters his prediction as we drift past the well-lit Amtrak station in Savannah, Georgia, and rumble over the Norfolk Southern diamond at Central Junction. There's just this one nagging thought I have. Five hours and 15 minutes into our trip from central Florida, P052, as CSX calls our train, is only 20 minutes off its unpublished schedule. Considering that a "heat order" the first three hours had slowed our pace from the usual 70 mph to 50, we're doing well. I say as much to King and the other engineer, David Phelps. King isn't buying it. He says that the worst is yet to come: "A couple of months ago, priorities seemed to change at CSX. Now they don't care about us."

Savannah River, 9:31 p.m. Yemassee, 10:05. Charleston, 10:57. On we go through the hot, muggy Georgia and Carolina night. Nothing holds us back. As we blitzkrieg Moncks Corner, South Carolina, at 11:17, King shouts over the din, "Starting about here, you begin having ugly meets." Sure enough, four minutes later, as we slow to cross the

Late on an afternoon in 2006, the *Auto Train* speeds through southern Virginia, its auto-carrying cars almost a blur of motion. *Fred W. Frailey*

Tail Race Canal drawbridge, there in the far distance is a locomotive headlight. "He's near St. Stephen," King remarks.

But between us and St. Stephen, South Carolina, are nothing but green signals, and in the siding sits a darkened Q173, the first of many southbound trains that usually block the *Auto Train's* path. Except that this night, we hold the main track and it does the waiting. What is going on? Q173 and its sister train, Q171, are the pride of the CSX A Line—intermodal trains used to stopping for no one (except maybe Q172 and Q174). The enginemen joke that CSX dispatchers know I'm aboard. But I don't think so.

Eighteen minutes after zipping past Q173, we get a "limited clear" signal at Santee Bluff, South Carolina, and diverge at 42 mph onto a stretch of double track. No sooner do we clear and begin to reaccelerate than K651 drifts past on the other track with a block of intermodal vans from Philadelphia in front of 40 empty Tropicana orange juice cars. K651 is a hot train. We've dodged two bullets so far.

It's almost midnight. Behind us, most of the lights are off in the passenger cars. People have turned in. I look at my watch, consult mileages in the Florence Division timetable, and reach a startling conclusion. "Guys," I say, "we could be on time into Florence." Florence, South Carolina, is 41 miles away and the crew-change point midway on the *Auto Train* route. Amtrak informally schedules P052 into Florence at 12:30. King agrees it could happen if Q171 doesn't stick us. He adds: "I don't think I've gotten to Florence by 12:30 in at least six months."

We would've made it, too, except that we slow to a crawl for a couple of minutes to let Q171 onto a double-track segment at New Hope, South Carolina. A bit later we streak by Q492, a Waycross, Georgia, to Hamlet, North Carolina, freight being held out of Florence, and round the sweeping curve into the station at 12:35, just as the southbound *Auto Train*, 65 minutes late, gets under way after its crew change.

While P42 locomotives 17 and 86 are refueled and a dining car watered, I wonder about the second half of this trip. The 299 miles from Florence to Richmond, Virginia, is typically where the *Auto Train* comes to grief. At Pembroke, North Carolina, 51 miles up the pike, we'll start seeing manifest trains that operate between northeastern cities and the classification yard at Hamlet. At Rocky Mount, North Carolina, train density picks up even more. The *Auto Train* almost never makes it through Richmond without some other train picking a fight with it.

The enginemen Lou Whitley and Eddie Liles climb aboard locomotive 17 and stow their stuff. Eddie takes first turn at the throttle. Because of making a second stop to water a second diner, we leave Florence 20 minutes late. Eddie has us at track speed, 70 mph, before we reach the north end of the Florence yard.

After leaving the Pee Dee River bottom, we go up and down the gentle coastal hills of the Carolinas. Liles and Whitley, like the other engineers I've met on the *Auto Train*, use "power braking" to prevent the auto carrier cars at the rear of the train from running in slack on the passenger cars. Power braking isn't done on other Amtrak trains, and freight railroads discourage or prohibit it because of brake-shoe wear, so the process bears describing: Starting over the crest of a hill at full throttle and doing, say, 65 mph, let up one or maybe two notches. If that doesn't check your speed (70 is all you're allowed), make an eight- or ten-pound air reduction so that the last auto carrier feels the pinch just as it reaches the top. Coming out of the dip and into the next hill, go back to full throttle and release the air as the first auto cars start climbing. Do this 100 or more times a night and you get good at it.

One more marquee train left to meet—P097, the southbound *Silver Meteor*. Nearing Cromartie, North Carolina, at 2:06 a.m., we get an approach limited signal (yellow over flashing green), telling us to slow to 45 mph or less before reaching the next signal, and then at the switch, a limited clear (red over flashing green), instructing us to take the turnout no faster than 45 mph and then resume speed. On the main track, barely moving, is the *Meteor*. We lose a mere four minutes.

But Eddie smells trouble. "Someone is running ahead of us," he says, pointing toward approach signals miles in front of us on the ruler-straight track. It could possibly be Q174, a Jacksonville-to-Boston intermodal train that left Jax four hours ahead of us. CSX dispatchers are notorious for making the *Auto Train* follow Q174. Both have 70-mph top speeds, but the *Auto Train* makes it over the road faster, if allowed. Our speculation is baseless. At Fayetteville, North Carolina, the culprit turns out to be an empty coal train, E555, which we easily slide around. It's 2:40 a.m., but we're now 25 minutes behind.

Our good fortune continues. Just north of Fayetteville, a southbound manifest clears for us, and our signal turns to green. At Wilson, North Carolina, a long northbound mixed freight is working the yard, but we dodge it on the other main track.

We cross over at South Elm City, North Carolina, to be out of the way of traffic entering or leaving Rocky Mount's yard just ahead. And in fact, southbound Q409 is leaving at 4:08 a.m. as we enter the terminal with the throttle still in notch eight, at 70 mph. Eddie begins braking near the yard office, where we see a trio of southbound freights that we won't have to contend with on the road. They're lined up side by side, waiting for us to go by. We pass the depot and former Atlantic Coast Line offices at a sedate 25 mph, just seven minutes off. Lorton remains about 200 miles away.

The next several hours pass in a blur. Lou takes over after Rocky Mount, while I fight to stay awake. We whip through little North Carolina and Virginia towns at the dawn of a warm, wet, overcast Sunday. Meanwhile, on the train, the kitchen staffs are laying out a continental breakfast for the 435 passengers.

We zip right through Richmond at 6:30 a.m., after being allowed to pass on Track 1 several northbound freights being held out on Track 2. As we do, I begin to hum the theme song from *Rocky*.

At 7:00 o'clock sharp, as occurs every morning on the *Auto Train*, its onboard manager turns on the PA system and updates passengers on our progress. What will he say this morning, as we push past the tiny community of Guinea? The only thing he can say: *We are on time!*

This is how it ends: Lou eases our train onto the lead track, stops for the yard crew to uncouple the 17 automobile cars on the rear (for the station switcher to grab), and then spots our 18 Superliners in front of the Lorton terminal building at 8:12 a.m., 18 minutes early. We are dumbstruck. What made it happen? Much later, I am told, through the back channel, that word had filtered up through CSX that I was aboard P052 and that the railroad put on its best behavior. Well, if I have to, I can live with the reputation of being a rainmaker.

March 2007 Trains

FORTY TWO

WHO *REALLY* SAVED ILLINOIS CENTRAL

I WANT TO MAKE AMENDS for an act of omission. In 2009 I wrote a feature story about Canadian National and its chief executive, Hunter Harrison. In describing Harrison's career, I said he had performed a "spectacular turnaround" at Illinois Central, starting in 1989 when he arrived from Burlington Northern as IC's operating vice president and then later as president. That's true, if you key on a few numbers. According to Moody's Investor Service, Harrison increased the profitability of the railroad by more than 700 percent in his first three years there. So far, so good.

But I implied that the Illinois Central before Harrison was a wrecked ship, and it was not. That was my act of omission. A friend recently sent me a privately published book, *Mentors and Memories: My Forty Years inside, outside and alongside the Railroad Industry.* Its author, Harry J. Bruce, is the real savior of the IC.

Bruce, age 81 as of this writing, came to the Illinois Central in 1975 as senior vice president of marketing. Before then, he had run Western Pacific's marketing department as a protégé of Alfred Perlman. Bruce was hired at IC by Alan Boyd, the railroad's president, who soon left. Boyd's successor, William Taylor, had been IC's Washington, DC, lobbyist, but as president, Bruce found Taylor ineffectual, because he did little to stem what Bruce saw as the railroad's two primary problems: too much track and too many people.

In April 1983, Taylor collapsed and died. Bruce replaced him. By then, Bruce relates in his book, he was convinced the railroad needed to be pruned virtually to its Chicago–New Orleans spine. But he didn't tell that to William Johnson, chairman of the railroad's holding company, because it was holy writ at IC that the railroad would be sold intact to some other entity, someday. The problem with sticking with the status quo was that IC was going broke. Operating profits peaked in 1974 and swung to deficits in 1979. The deficits were growing year by year. Goldman Sachs told the railroad in that period it couldn't expect to fetch more than $250–300 million in a sale.

Illinois Central Gulf, as the railroad was then known, was saddled with worn-out lines largely inherited from IC's 1972 merger with the lightly trafficked Gulf, Mobile & Ohio. Bruce's idea was simplicity itself: sell the appendages in packages to nonunion startup companies. Together, they would fetch at least $250 million and leave IC with its profitable north-south core, the only part of IC where traffic had not degraded in the past 30 years. It's true that something like this had been done during the formation of Conrail, but that was a government-run operation. This was a private railroad acting to save itself.

In hindsight, Bruce's plan was diabolically smart. He and a fellow executive, the late Doug Hagestad, approached the sales like a marketing project. Initially, they created four packages of rail lines to sell, for perhaps $275 million. Then someone leaked word of this to the *Chicago Tribune* (hint hint). Bruce gladly confirmed the facts, and (by his telling) people began breaking down the doors to make offers. In all, the line sales brought in $450 million. This cut IC's revenue in half. But, lo and behold, the losses ended, IC became profitable again, and a large part of its debt was repaid. Nobody ever downsized a sick railroad better than Harry Bruce.

But that wasn't all Bruce did. "Every inspection trip made it clearer and clearer that the way the work was organized and the assignments divided up was being driven by the number of employees available rather than by the amount and type of work," Bruce wrote. Managers knew which employees were productive and which were not. Bruce came up with a plan, little used in railroading at the time, of offering job buyouts to selected employees. They would be called into their supervisors' offices and offered a check, already cut, equal to one year's salary, for which the railroad would pay the income tax. To be given that check, they had to resign immediately.

Overwhelmingly, employees accepted the buyouts, because younger workers could take the money and get a new job, and older workers could pay off home mortgages and maintain their standard of living on less income.

From line sales and buyouts, the head count at IC went from 9,887 in 1984 to 3,164 five years later. In the next several years, the rest of the railroad industry, having learned from Harry Bruce, adopted buyouts to solve the most intractable dispute in labor union history: crew sizes. The face of railroading was starkly changed.

So that's the part of the story I left out in 2009. Harry Bruce's contributions to his industry are, in my opinion, underappreciated. Not all the railroads created by those line sales succeeded, but over time their impact was to create value where little or none existed before, while strengthening the railroad that remained. And while eliminating jobs is an uncomfortable task, not eliminating unneeded jobs is a sure route to failure, and buyouts certainly reduced the pain for those affected.

Thank you, Harry, and I apologize it took so long to say so.

September 2013 Trains

FORTY THREE

WHY YOU MAY YET READ BY CANDLELIGHT

THE DEBATE OVER THE SAFETY of handling crude oil by rail has become frustrating and almost pointless. Yes, tank cars that carry oil could be made more crashworthy—that is, if the Pipeline and Hazardous Materials Safety Administration would get off its duff and tell tank car owners what changes it wants. A year after the tragedy in Lac-Mégantic, Quebec, that killed 47 people, we're still waiting. Yes, there are a couple of other measures that would make a marginal difference. But if you're asking whether railroads will ever make their trains absolutely, totally safe and derailment-free, the answer is no, of course not. So what's this all about?

Almost everything you do in life comes with risk. When you shave, you risk a cut. When you eat, you risk indigestion or worse. In 2012, 33,561 people died in roadway accidents, a number that to me seems horrifying. And I tense up every time a jetliner I'm in takes off and lands. Still, nobody suggests that you not shave or eat or drive or fly. Instead, we try to make all these activities safer. For instance, railroads are investing $13 billion over a period of years to install positive train control, which will prevent trains from passing red signals or violating speed limits, even temporary slow orders.

But in the public debate, rational thought doesn't seem to matter. I hate to pick on Sara Foss, a columnist for the *Daily Gazette* of Schenectady, New York, because she had nice things to say about a feature story I wrote this year. On the other hand, in a blog of hers she so well illustrates the problem that I cannot help myself. First, she asks the wrong question: "Can transporting oil by rail ever truly be made safe?" Truly? It's the wrong question because absolute safety is just as impossible on a railroad as it is on the highway and in the air. Then, for an answer to her pointless question, Sara goes, inexplicitly, to Sandy Steubing, a member of People of Albany United for Safe Energy, or PAUSE. It's like asking Barack Obama whether George W. Bush will go down as one of our greatest presidents. As if on cue, Steubing demands a moratorium on shipping crude oil via both rail *and* pipeline so that the U.S. can "aggressively switch to renewable forms of energy." And Sara agrees with him, perhaps mindless of the shortage of gasoline that will result.

Give Sandy Steubing credit for at least being honest. Too many others in the environmental movement are disingenuous. Told that absolute safety for crude by rail is unachievable, they say then just stop the activity. It's a mind-set that if applied the same way to the other forms of transportation would have us all reduced to riding bicycles, living in caves, and reading by candlelight. The fact of the matter is that these people don't want the oil to come out of the ground, period. But they don't want to say that aloud.

It's not just the environmentalists, either. The oil industry denies against all evidence that there is anything unusually volatile about light sweet crude oil from North Dakota and says it's all a railroad problem. And the pipeline and environmental people talk right past each other, too (while railroads walk off with the business, I might add).

On that last note, here's another example of the mindlessness of it all. Reported the *New York Times* in early June: "If the Keystone XL pipeline is not built—and more oil from the Canadian oil sands is moved by rail—there could be hundreds more deaths and thousands more injuries than expected over the course of a decade, according to an updated State Department analysis." Specifically, State predicts 434 deaths and 2,947 injuries over a decade. The *Times* reporter got reactions from a TransCanada spokesman ("The safest, most environmentally responsible way to move oil to the markets where they are needed is a pipeline") and from an attorney for the National Wildlife Federation ("Today's correction further highlights the extreme dangers to people and wildlife posed by climate-disrupting tar sands oil"). But nobody from the *Times* sought comment from the railroad industry.

It took an enterprising young reporter for the McClatchy Newspapers, Curtis Tate, to reveal that State's estimates had nothing to do with the dangers of hauling crude oil by rail—nothing whatever. The stats were simply lifted from the Federal Railroad Administration (FRA) website and represent the casualties per million ton-miles of freight of any kind handled during 2002–2012 and extrapolated over the next decade. Most of those casualties probably involved grade crossing accidents and incidents having to do with trespassers. On top of that, the rate of accidents and injuries on railroads has declined by almost half during the past decade, so even these statistics are exaggerated.

Let me present a few statistics of my own. A couple of months ago I did some back-of-the-envelope calculations, consulted FRA safety stats, and concluded that over a year's time, we will probably have 11 crude oil train incidents—a statistical probability, in other words, at the rate that oil is being hauled by rail today. Only half would involve loaded trains, obviously. So are five or six derailments per year, minor or not minor (because who knows?), a risk this nation can take and work around? Before you answer no, let me remind you of two other statistics. They are the number of people in the United States killed and injured the past year in crude oil derailments. Those numbers are zero and zero.

So if I seem impatient with the public dialogue, at least you now know why.

June 19, 2014 TrainsMag.com

—ᴍ—

14TH STREET AT NIGHT

AMTRAK'S 14TH STREET COACH YARD in Chicago is a city within the city, a matrix of tracks, buildings, compressed-air pipes, and motorized 480-volt power harnesses. Even so, from Roosevelt Road, your destination sticks out like a beacon. Amid all those silver-sided passenger cars, only one is clothed in Pullman green. Santa Fe business car 56 was built in 1923 and served the railway's general managers and vice presidents faithfully for more than half a century. When he'd made a success of the Indiana Rail Road, Tom Hoback made a present to himself of car 56, buying it in 2004 from BNSF Railway. Its interior today looks unchanged from when it was a traveling office. For the son of a Santa Fe chief dispatcher, it is just this side of heaven.

You sit down for drinks with Tom and Jack Barriger, a retired Santa Fe lifer. Outside, as light begins to fade, BNSF dinkies and Amtrak intercity trains scoot by every so often a dozen tracks away. Inside, a railroad radio murmurs in the background. The conversation turns to Fred Gurley, in many respects the father of the modern Santa Fe. Raised in humble circumstances, he nonetheless became a Burlington Lines division superintendent by age 31.

As he rose through the ranks at the Q and later Santa Fe (lured there by its president, Edward Engle, in 1939), Gurley preached the gospel of change. He once remarked that he preferred a diesel locomotive cab to a business car because it showed him where he was going rather than where he'd been. He personally supervised the record-breaking, dawn-to-dusk run of the *Pioneer Zephyr* from Denver to Chicago in 1934. At Santa Fe, as its VP of operations, Gurley had 30 four-unit sets of FT freight diesels in service across the western desert before World War II. At war's end he resumed ordering diesels as fast as the builders could deliver them while equipping the *Chiefs* with 623 streamlined passenger cars. The brand new *San Francisco Chief* (1954) and high-level *El Capitan* (1956) came on Gurley's 15-year watch as president and then chief executive. You see, once upon a time you could make the case that passenger trains made money. For sure, they made reputations. In the Gurley era, 1944–1959, Santa Fe became synonymous with high quality.

The three of you are at the dinner table now, the eastbound *Cardinal* and *Capitol Limited* having gone past your windows earlier. Jack's job in 1971 was to dispose of Santa Fe's passenger car fleet. By then, Fred Gurley had been retired for a dozen years but still maintained an office in Santa Fe's Chicago headquarters.

Cutting into his steak, Barriger relates Gurley's intense interest in the car sale. He asked Jack to drop by his apartment near the Loop. There, they spoke for more than two hours. Although Jack doesn't say so, you infer that Gurley was bothered, even depressed. And why not be? This was his legacy to the Santa Fe being sacrificed to jet aircraft and interstate highways. He gave his railroad the finest trains in the land, and look at them now, he must have thought.

Had he still been in a position to influence events, Gurley at the very least would have tried to sell Amtrak on the virtues of Santa Fe's 21st Street Coach Yard, versus Penn Central's 14th Street, as a new home. Whereas 14th Street then was a physical wreck, 21st Street remained in excellent condition. It's fair to assume that the quality of Santa Fe's workforce was superior to Penn Central's. But it was not to be. A year ago you tried to find where 21st Street had stood, but it's largely buried beneath an expanded Chinatown.

Under arc lights, you take a long walk along the platforms of 14th Street. Your yearning for the smell of sweet diesel exhaust is fully satisfied. The yard today hardly resembles PC's ramshackle facility of four decades ago. Everything appears new, from welded rail to the two-track inspection building that can hold entire Superliner trains. A huge office structure is topped by a spacious control tower. All the tracks are neatly ballasted with small, boot-friendly rock.

Back inside car 56, sipping red wine, the three of you debate who among Santa Fe's leaders deserves to head the pack. A student of Santa Fe history, Tom favors William Barstow Strong (president 1881–1889), who pushed the railroad over the Rockies and into California. Jack credits Gurley with moving a beaten-up Santa Fe to the front ranks of western railroads, prepared to be the company his dad envisioned in the book *Super-Railroads for a Dynamic American Economy.* But the best? He's uncertain. You're hung up between Ed Ripley (1895–1920) and Rob Krebs (1987–1995), a decisive duo who got Santa Fe over rough patches. Discussions like this never get settled, do they?

At 11:00 o'clock the three of you look up to see a visitor. A young yard conductor is on the rear platform, releasing the hand brake. Presently a P32 in switching service couples on and takes you to the rear of tomorrow's *Empire Builder,* which is poking out of the inspection house. The whole train is pulled south and then shoved north to a track on the east side of the yard, to await the next afternoon's departure.

Tonight you've gone from present to past and back many times. Tom pulls down the shades of car 56. Safe and secure inside a symbol of Santa Fe's glorious past and surrounded by Amtrak's uncertain present, the three of you call it a day.

February 2012 Trains

—⟋m⟍—

THE WRECK OF OLD 54

MY TALE BEGINS AT THE breakfast table on a gorgeous autumn morning, Wednesday, October 12, 1955. I'm 11 years old. My big sister Carolyn and I are getting ready for school. The phone rings. It's my dad, who not 15 minutes earlier left for work at the daily newspaper he owns and edits. Mom listens, hangs up, and turns to me: "Your father said to tell you that two L&A freight trains collided head on this morning. East of town a few miles. There was a huge fire but nobody is dead, yet. He's trying to rent a plane to get an aerial photo. That's all he knows now."

Let's put this in context. Sulphur Springs, Texas, is a town then of 9,000 people, 80 miles east of Dallas. Nothing ever happens here; even murders over love triangles are a decade apart. This, however, is national news. To me, it's as if a spaceship from Saturn had set down three miles from 835 Ardis Street. Trains aren't just part of my life in 1955. They are my life. I care not for school, for girls, for small talk, or for what I'll do when I grow up. All that matters is railroads, and I soak up information like a sponge. Yes, I drive my family crazy.

After school, I pedal furiously to the end of Whitworth Street and then walk a mile along the tracks. What a mess. What we call "the L&A" is really the Texas Subdivision of Kansas City Southern Railway, extending from Shreveport, Louisiana, to Dallas. Seven of the eight red, yellow, and black F units are splayed across the right-of-way, several on their sides, as are 23 freight cars. Big derricks, one from Shreveport and the other from Minden, Louisiana, are already at work,

This 1955 disaster in northeast Texas occurred because a telegrapher misunderstood a dispatcher and deleted the wrong train order. *Fred W. Frailey collection*

picking their way toward each other through the mess, each derrick tethered to a black GP7. I see track workers constructing a shoofly around the wreckage so that service can be restored. I also see railroad officials wearing cheap suits, neckties, and, of course, fedoras.

But strangely, nobody restricts my access to the wreckage. I walk right up to the giant, silent locomotives. They reek of spilled diesel fuel, which to me has the same fragrance as a rose. One of the lead diesels is half buried in dirt. I look directly down into the engineer's side of the cab and see his grip. All six people aboard the engines jumped before the collision, one of them critically hurt when his head struck a culvert. Was it the person whose bag I see? I reach in the grip and pick up a time book inscribed with a man's name, Long. Immediately I feel guilty. I look around, spot one of the fedoras, and give him the book. He thanks me and suggests I not get so close to the wreckage.

At dinner that evening, Pop explains there was a "lap order." That is, one train (No. 54) got orders to meet the other at Brashear, 7 miles west of Sulphur Springs, whereas the second train (Extra 76 South) was told to meet 54 at Como, 9 miles east of town. Their rights overlapped, in other words, and they came to grief halfway between the two sidings.

Let's reconstruct that evening. Train 54, headed toward Dallas, pauses at Hughes Springs to set off and pick up cars. There it gets train order 96, issued at 9:40 p.m., which reads: "No 54 Eng 73 meet Extra 76 South at Como." The rear brakeman on 54, William Daum, recollected in a 2011 statement that his conductor thought Brashear, on the other side of Sulphur Springs, would make a better meeting place and asked the Hughes Springs telegrapher to so inform the train dispatcher, G. H. Bland. Bland must have accepted that advice, because at 10:09 p.m. he issues order 97: "No 54 Eng 73 meet Extra 76 South at Brashear instead of Como."

These two orders, read together, are perfectly straightforward. The second order supersedes the first and sets Brashear as the new meeting point. Both orders are delivered to train 54, which leaves Hughes Springs at 10:25 p.m. Daum never feels the emergency brakes at 12:40 a.m. before the train suddenly stops. The collision site is chaotic. Fire trucks are trying to reach the burning wreckage. Neighbors search for crew members. A man living nearby finds the engineer of Extra

76 South, "Flappy" Long, entangled in the stirrup of the ladder from locomotive 76's cab, his elbow and shoulder fractured.

Why did Extra 76 South go past the new meeting point at Brashear? Because it never received order 97! Here is what happened: Dispatcher Bland issued order 95 to the telegraphers at Hughes Springs and Hunt Yard in Greenville, which created a work extra in the vicinity of Hughes Springs. The work extra tied up, so Bland issued order 106 addressed to the same telegraphers that read: "Order No. 95 is annulled." But the telegrapher at Hunt Yard wrote as follows: "Order No 97 is annulled." Both operators repeated the order back to Bland as copied, and neither Bland nor the Hughes Springs operator caught the error. And when the Hunt Yard operator read to Bland the train orders to be delivered to Extra 76 South, Bland did not notice that order 97 was not among them but order 95 was.

The rules that govern railroad operations are written in blood, it is said. In other words, we learn from our mistakes and refine the rules. But short of positive train control (once it is implemented), there is no fail-safe rule against compound human errors. Thus, the wreck of Old 54.

December 2015 Trains

FORTY SIX

THE MOTHER OF ALL TRAFFIC JAMS

Well, another fine mess we've gotten ourselves into. With all the sidings west of Houston blocked except Harlem and Weimar. There's a IHOLBB 01 tied up on the east main, a crew patching the ADOHO back into Houston, MTUHO 25 tied up in the Ballpark, ILAAV 27 tied up on the west main with a switch crew on, IAVLB and OGKBM called out, with a IDOHO 27 that hogs at 10:45 and a MCCHO coming. . . . Guess nobody knows what the hell is going on.

—Corridor manager's report, Harriman
Dispatching Center, October 2, 1997

MELTDOWNS ON US RAILROADS WEREN'T invented yesterday. The government seized the rails during World War I when service collapsed under the strain. More recently, in 1979, paralysis of its Houston terminal shut down Southern Pacific from Jonesboro, Arkansas, to West Colton, California; SP folks called it their World War III. Burlington Northern in 1984 shelled out more than $1 million for taxis to rescue crews of coal trains whose allowable working hours had expired on its threadbare Alliance Division. And remember Penn Central?

But for sheer size and catastrophic consequences, nothing since the presidency of Woodrow Wilson matches the mother of all coagulations that settled in on the industry giant Union Pacific during the second half of 1997.

Problems began in earnest in Houston last spring, and in only a couple of weeks they almost paralyzed traffic on former SP lines there. Unable to get in, freight trains by the score tied up in sidings leading to Houston. But trains ready to depart couldn't leave because the locomotives they needed were on the trains that couldn't get in. By July, the effects reached Fort Worth, and it went down, too. (The head-on collision that killed two railroaders at UP's Centennial Yard in Fort Worth on August 20 involved runaway light engines off an inbound train from El Paso that was tied up west of Fort Worth.)

Shreveport . . . Pine Bluff . . . West Colton . . . Council Bluffs. The operational disease spread outward, feeding upon Union Pacific's resources. Its 6,200-unit locomotive fleet, newest in the nation, was sucked into the quagmire, short-changing trains on the rest of the 36,000-mile railroad, and schedules went to the dogs. Crews were in short supply. Predictably, by September hardly a portion of the property remained unaffected. One morning, Bailey Yard in North Platte, Nebraska, on UP's 120-train-a-day coal corridor and transcontinental main line, awoke to find itself 161 locomotives short of the number needed to power trains expected to leave during the following 24 hours. On the morning of October 8, systemwide, 550 freights stood still for lack of engines or crews. As Edward Emmett of the National Industrial Transportation League, a shippers' group, told the *Journal of Commerce*: "It's almost like the old buffalo hunts. We have carcasses of trains all over the West."

And such a sight it was: Trains with loaded cars sat for a week at a stretch in such locales as Missouri City and Tyler, Texas, and Picacho and Shawmut, Arizona. Other trains consumed two and even three weeks reaching their destinations. Incompatible computer systems of the formerly independent Union Pacific and Southern Pacific, seemingly impervious to human interdiction, directed loaded cars hither and yon around the Southwest—anywhere but the siding of the consignee. And the new UP chairman, Richard K. Davidson, had to explain why the mayhem UP vowed would never occur were it allowed to buy rival Southern Pacific had come to pass anyway, in spades.

Amid all this, Union Pacific trains kept colliding. On October 25, intermodal train IHOLB slid through the end of double track at West

Junction, in Houston, and struck Tucson-Houston manifest MTUHO head on, igniting a spectacular fire. Four days later and 70 miles to the northeast, train MNPHO from North Platte smashed into the rear of a standing unit rock train at Navasota, Texas, at 25 mph. Evidence strongly suggested that the engineer and conductor of MNPHO who had gone on duty four hours earlier, at midnight after a mere eight hours' rest, were asleep. Luckily, no one was seriously hurt in either collision. But the wrecks prompted the second full-press safety blitz by the Federal Railroad Administration in a month. Said a tired and depressed UP yardmaster in Houston: "We're a dangerous railroad right now."

To its credit, UP soon announced a "guaranteed time off plan" for stressed Texas crews. Still, it was enough to make you wonder: How could such a mess possibly have happened?

> All need to be aware, any train with power not moving within 24 hours after being parked becomes a candidate to have the power stripped and run off of our region, leaving the cars and blocked siding for us to deal with. Need to do all possible to "push" the terminals to take the inbounds. Do not hesitate to mention this fact when dealing with them!
>
> Corridor director's report, Harriman Dispatching Center,
> October 11, 1997

Union Pacific's official explanation of what went wrong in Texas— "the best judgment of UP/SP's senior operating officials"—was contained in a report in August 1997 to the Surface Transportation Board, the agency that succeeded the Interstate Commerce Commission. The railroad cited these reasons:

Track work on the Sunset Route. As part of the SP merger deal, Burlington Northern Santa Fe in December 1996 bought the 200 miles of ex-SP track west of New Orleans, on which UP kept trackage rights; starting in April, BNSF slapped a curfew on train movements for parts of each day as tie and bridge gangs went to work. On the portion east of Houston that UP kept, 100,000 ties were replaced, too, with attendant curfews.

Service interruptions. During the spring, UP experienced a spate of derailments and weather catastrophes on former SP lines in Texas. A freight derailed at Rison, on the old Cotton Belt Route. Flash floods took out the Sunset Route at Hondo, west of San Antonio. Two derailments occurred in Englewood Yard, SP's big facility in Houston. Then in June two trains collided at Devine, south of San Antonio on the UP Laredo line, apparently due to a dispatcher's error.

Border chaos. UP's San Antonio–Laredo line handles 80 percent of US–Mexico rail traffic. During the two weeks before Mexico's Northeast rail concession was privatized on June 23 (to an affiliate of Kansas City Southern), backups on both sides of the border grew. As many as 11 trains were stored on Union Pacific waiting to cross the Rio Grande.

Surge in plastics. Shippers may store cars after they are loaded with plastic pellets, and in fact there's an entire yard devoted to "storage in transit" (SIT) near Houston. But SIT volume became so heavy it began eating into space in other yards. On one day, five trainloads of SIT cars left Houston on ex-SP lines, to make room for others.

Disruptions on CSX. In July, Hurricane Danny devastated CSX tracks and bridges northeast of New Orleans, causing connecting UP trains to detour to CSX at Memphis. Also, CSX put a 250-person rail gang to work on its New Orleans route, causing more backups.

In addition, Union Pacific people wasted no opportunity to disparage SP's physical shape at the time of the September 1996 merger. Moreover, although the two railroads are united in theory, they won't be one in fact until their employees work together and their computers talk alike. "Hub" labor agreements allowing crews to run on any line radiating from Houston, Pine Bluff, North Little Rock, San Antonio, and Dallas–Fort Worth, regardless of the heritage of those routes, either haven't been negotiated and ratified by union members or are still qualifying crews over unfamiliar territories. And the cutover in Texas from SP's computers to UP's wasn't to occur until December.

All these explanations for failure, while undoubtedly true, are unconvincing. They portray Union Pacific as victim, a virtuous railroad suffering from forces it cannot control. Nowhere do you see the words: "Folks, we screwed up." So you have to wonder whether you're getting the whole story. Extensive interviews with railroaders within and without Union Pacific but in every case close to the ground in Texas suggest additional explanations:

Operating changes. Englewood Yard freezes up when you cram it for very long with more than 3,500 cars or when you constantly classify more than 1,700 cars a day over its hump. Southern Pacific learned in 1979 that when Englewood tilts, you may as well hang an Out of Business sign at its entrance. Cash-starved SP worked around Englewood's limitations several ways. First, every conceivable car went around rather than through the yard. Avondale Yard in New Orleans and West Colton Yard in California made up solid Avondale-West Colton trains that sped through Houston, bypassing Englewood Yard. Unit grain trains were sent straight to Houston's Port Terminal Railroad Association.

More important, two satellite yards processed most of the chemical cars. Strang, 22 miles southeast of Englewood on the Galveston Line, used its 12-track minihump to make up 10,000-ton chemical trains for East St. Louis, Memphis, and New Orleans, and to distribute empties. It was enormously efficient, humping about 900 cars a day and being emptied every 12 hours, first by 11 switchers that ply industries along the Houston Ship Channel and second by outbound loaded trains of tank cars and covered hoppers. Closer to Englewood, Dayton Yard served seven road switchers on the Baytown Line and preblocked cars to be picked up by passing trains, thus avoiding Englewood.

Third, SP relied on block swapping among trains to get them sorted out on the road rather than in the terminals. Houston, Strang, and Beaumont, for example, might send a train with cars for mixed destinations in the same direction in close order. Down the line they swapped blocks of cars, to form solid trains for three destinations—for East St. Louis, Memphis, and Pine Bluff, in this instance.

All these workarounds appalled Union Pacific management. UP's style is to process all cars in big, low-cost yards and to send forth full trains for a single destination. And if the task proves daunting—if your yard begins to choke waiting for those solid trains to accumulate—you simply quit your sniveling, take a deep breath, say a Hail Mary, and do the job by brute force, never giving up.

So sometime last spring UP moved outbound classification of cars from both Strang and Dayton yards to Englewood, to get things done the right (UP) way. Results were utterly predictable. "Trains began backing up the next day," reports a senior Englewood yardmaster. Adding hundreds more cars to the 1,500 to 1,700 Englewood already classified was like throwing lit matches on a powder keg. *Trains* learned of numerous attempts by persons intimately familiar with Englewood Yard to dissuade UP. For example, the head of a connecting railroad said to the Southern Region general manager, Charles Malone, "You're getting ready to sink this." Perhaps because some of these warnings came from former employees now working for other railroads, they were ignored. Says Davidson: "Obviously, the Strang thing didn't work. Their hearts were in the right place, because they wanted to handle the business more efficiently. But it was more than Englewood could deal with."

For his part, Malone says the changes occurred after an extensive study of car flows through the three yards. Moreover, he says, he had assurances from people running Englewood and Strang—themselves former Southern Pacific officers—that it would work.

Slow reactions. The Houston Service Unit chief, Gregg Garrison, says the yard consolidation was "the beginning of what got us behind." In months since, Englewood has never emptied enough to catch its breath. Davidson thinks the diversion of traffic from Strang and Dayton yards only lasted 10 days. "My boys down there tell me we'd recovered from that substantially before other things occurred that put us over the edge again," the chairman says. But UP employees in Houston say the arrangement lasted almost a month and was never really undone. Strang assembles half its former number of through trains, while the other chemical cars are still classified at Englewood, which on October 27 held 6,179 cars, far above its comfortable capacity.

A veteran dispatcher whose territory covers the heart of Houston sees a lack of leadership. "Nobody knows what to do to fix it," he says. "They hold conferences and reach decisions and then never reveal the decisions to those of us who must carry them out." Added Dennis Duffy, a senior vice president of UP, to an internal gathering: "We really thought we could isolate this to Texas but found it was all interrelated." Thus, Duffy said, this Texas barbeque began to cook the whole railroad.

Hubris. According to former SP officers, their new UP bosses aren't much interested in their opinions about what will work on ex-SP tracks and what won't. One man who cautioned Malone about Houston yard consolidations says the general manager replied it would work because "we've got the people who can make it work and the resources of Union Pacific." Conceded UP's Duffy to his colleagues: "We have had a reputation for being somewhat arrogant."

Yes, and arrogant in a manner that gets in the way of solving problems. Just compare how UP reacted to this meltdown with Southern Pacific's approach to its own Englewood coagulation in 1979. "I'd have hit Houston with a sledgehammer," Davidson said in October. But Union Pacific's hammer blows were misaimed. Starting in August 1997, it sent hundreds of managers to Texas, primarily to act as train crews. Another 150 engineers signed up from other parts of the railroad. But they treated symptoms, not causes. Only in October did the railroad begin to address problems in a systemic fashion. And Southern Pacific? In December 1979, their general manager, Bill Lacy, simply ordered 1,500 cars destined for Houston destinations taken out of Englewood and shoved down the Bellaire Line main track, to be retrieved later, so transcontinental traffic could flow through. Crude, but it gave Englewood breathing room. Sure, Lacy angered a lot of customers in Houston. But so did UP in 1997.

> Western boys slammed the door shut at Yuma just before noon account ran totally out of crews. Supposed to be something like 26 crews laying off between Yuma and West Colton. Not calling any more west out of Alpine [Texas] on account of this.
>
> Corridor director's report, Harriman Dispatching Center,
> October 5, 1997

Near the height of the disorder, on October 1, Union Pacific presented a "service recovery plan" that evolved from almost two weeks of soul searching by top officers. The scope of this plan seemed as encompassing as the congestion that spawned it. At the time, the railroad held

45,000 more freight cars on the property than six months earlier—the equivalent of a line of standing cars more than 500 miles long. In the meantime, its average train speed had plunged from 18 mph to 12.5 mph, which equates to a loss of 1,800 locomotives, or more than a fourth of the fleet. To get back on its feet, UP began these short-term initiatives:

Fewer trains. Several trains, including intermodal schedules, were combined. Texas Mexican Railway hauled Houston–Laredo trains (using crowded ex-SP tracks east of Corpus Christi), as did the South Orient Railroad between Alpine in West Texas and Fort Worth. On a larger scale, Kansas City Southern took over UP's unit grain trains between Kansas City and Houston, and Beaumont, Port Allen, and Mexico, in conjunction with KCS affiliate Tex-Mex. Iowa Interstate and Illinois Central operated some UP trains between Council Bluffs and Chicago. Even UP spinoff Missouri & Northern Arkansas moved empty coal trains from Newport, Arkansas, where it intersects UP's St. Louis–Texas main, to Pleasant Hill, Missouri, east of Kansas City.

Reroutes. Numerous internal detours were set up to keep trains out of Houston and central Texas. Example: New Orleans–Long Beach intermodal trains INOLB and ILBNO skipped Houston by traveling the entire former Texas & Pacific route via Shreveport, Fort Worth, and Big Spring. An Atlanta–Long Beach train operated in conjunction with Norfolk Southern east of Memphis detoured north to St. Louis and then west to Kansas City and Tucumcari, New Mexico, before intersecting its original route at El Paso.

Suspended services. Union Pacific temporarily ended its own intermodal trains between Chicago and Texas (United Parcel Service already had taken its business on this lane to BNSF) and substituted a train between Chicago and Houston routed over NS and KCS; its roundabout trek took it from Chicago to Fort Wayne, Chattanooga, Birmingham, Meridian, Shreveport, and Beaumont before ending up in Houston.

Rent-a-yard. Texarkana took on some switching performed by Centennial Yard in Fort Worth. Alexandria, Louisiana, processed some 300 cars per day for Settegast, UP's premerger yard in Houston. Coffeyville, Kansas, assumed work done by North Little Rock. Parsons, Kansas (going south), and Waco, Texas (going north), classified

a total of 5 trains that Fort Worth would otherwise handle on the former Missouri-Kansas-Texas route. In Houston, the Port Terminal
made up two daily trains to run directly to Pine Bluff, avoiding Englewood and Settegast. Even the short lines Georgetown Railroad, Fort
Worth & Western, and Texas City Terminal signed on to switch UP's
traffic.

All this, of course, was in addition to a hiring and promotion spree
that UP had hoped to avoid, because the hub-and-spoke crewing
planned for major cities should, when put in place, bring great efficien-
cies in use of train crew. The goal of the recovery plan was to restore
UP's northern lines to premeltdown functionality by the end of October and the southern part of the railroad by the end of 1997.

Union Pacific's recovery plan seemed to effectively address everything but the Houston terminal problem that lay at the core of its
troubles.

> MSRASK 15 had all engines crap out around Nacogdoches. Had to
> cut off and get the power off a train at Appleby and will go to Paxton
> and tie up, also killing the MHOPB and MBTPB, which are behind
> him and further eating into the crew base.
>
> Corridor director's report, Harriman Dispatching Center,
> October 17, 1997

Reports to November 3 were inconclusive but encouraging. The
jackpot around Houston dissolved (but kept reforming because Englewood's car count remained astronomical). Fewer trains waited for
locomotives (but more waited for crews). The inventory of cars on line
fell by 14,000 during October to 342,000, a hopeful omen.

On Friday, October 17, the railroad is a study in contrasts. Englewood Yard is getting trains out and dog-catch crews are emptying sidings west of town of stalled trains. Two weeks earlier, 40 trains were
held out of Fort Worth, but today only 10. At the start of the month,
2,000 cars hadn't moved in two or more days; today the count is 1,000
and falling.

Now West Colton, 80 miles east of Los Angeles, is the terminal
needing last rites. Thirteen westbound freights sit on sidings between

Colton and the Arizona border at Yuma, leaving only one open siding between Ferrum and Glamis, 60 miles, on which to meet trains.
Matters are even worse to the east. Seventeen westbounds are parked
between Yuma and Tucson, Arizona, eight of them nose to tail on a
stretch of double track starting 20 miles east of Yuma. But this is progress. A few days earlier, 54 West Colton–bound trains were waylaid
in sidings as far away as Texas and Kansas. Still, Amtrak's eastbound
Sunset Limited tonight will be tortured, hit for an hour of delay from
LA to Palm Springs and then three more hours to Yuma as it gets in
line behind eastbound freights. The *Sunset* will reach New Orleans
12 hours behind schedule.

Now swing back to Texas. On the hilly Rabbit Line from Houston to Shreveport and north on the former Cotton Belt to Pine Bluff
(415 miles) are 31 sidings, and by midafternoon of the seventeenth, 18
of them hold stalled trains or strings of waylaid freight cars. And in
the next week there will be little improvement. Four days later, the
Southern Corridor manager in Omaha reports to his relief: "Have no
crews at Pine Bluff to run trains north. Engineers are hiding and not
taking calls. Really ugly at this time. You will see intermodal trains
tied down account can't run out of Pine Bluff." South of Shreveport
wasn't much better: "MHOPB lost one engine and will have to tie up
at Leggett. Won't hurt because there are three trains stopped ahead
of him anyway." On October 24 it rained so hard on the Rabbit that
engineers couldn't see in front of their locomotives, and everything
ground to a halt.

Finally, on October 25, two days before a Surface Transportation
Board hearing in Washington, the Union Pacific side agrees for two
days to run five trains that would normally go up the SP side to Pine
Bluff, into North Little Rock instead. Meanwhile, UP can scarcely
meet trains on its Houston–Brownsville line because 17 of 19 sidings
are plugged. But Davidson, at 10:34 a.m. on October 27, is able to tell
the STB hearing that only one train is waylaid between Houston and
Pine Bluff.

Steve Barkley has said that our main corridors must be cleaned
up by Monday. For us on the Southern, this would be Pine Bluff

to Houston. Dick Davidson is scheduled to testify before the STB on Monday about the progress we are making on the service recovering plan.

Corridor director's report, Harriman Dispatching Center,
October 25, 1997

Sometimes big events turn on a hunch. Although the railroad's service recovery plan set a goal of December 31 to returning the property to prechaos normalcy, Davidson had told his executives he wanted it fixed sooner. So when questioned by STB chairman Linda Morgan at the start of a 12-hour hearing in Washington, he decides on the spot to go public with an earlier deadline. "We are essentially back on track on the northern tier," Davidson says. "I will be terribly disappointed if this isn't back to normal by Thanksgiving or very shortly thereafter. That's my goal." A few minutes later he repeats: "It will be substantially fixed within thirty days." In other words, he implies, why involve government when we're well on the way toward a solution?

Thereupon, Davidson sits attentively for ten hours, silently absorbing blows few CEOs ever endure: public damnation by dozens of big customers. "Some cars are taking two weeks just to leave Houston," complains Joe Alderman of Texas Petrochemical Corp. Declares Don Olsen of Huntsman Corp.: "We cannot ship with confidence on Union Pacific." DuPont's Hugh Fischer says railroads as a group "are quickly deteriorating into a national disaster." Yet despite their anger, the shippers remain divided over what to do. Some want government-ordered relief, while others believe UP should be given more time.

A lot may hinge on what one of the last witnesses has to say. He's the BNSF chairman, Robert Krebs, who spends the entire day three rows behind Davidson, intently watching the denunciations of his rival company. He and Davidson don't chat during breaks that day, but when Krebs finally gets his chance, he never even mentions BNSF's own plan to encroach upon UP traffic and tracks or its desire to dispatch the Rabbit and Cotton Belt as far north as Memphis. Instead comes this: "Dick has pledged every resource the Union Pacific has to straighten this out. They ought to have a chance. I don't know what the magic number is . . . thirty or forty-five days." Davidson later says he was as surprised as anyone else at Krebs's support. "But you know," the UP chief adds, "it could be he thought BNSF would have trouble making good if it got what it asked for."

Four days later the STB takes the minimalist approach. It stops far short of giving competitors open access to UP customers. Tex-Mex gets rights to serve customer under contract to UP who are switched by the Houston Port Terminal Railroad or Houston Belt & Terminal (itself about to be divided among co-owners BNSF and UP). Tex-Mex also gets a more direct route to its own Corpus Christi–Laredo tracks, via Union Pacific's signaled Brownsville Subdivision. (The little railroad already holds trackage rights on UP east of Houston to reach half owner KCS at Beaumont, as well as rights over the former SP via Flatonia and Victoria to Corpus Christi.)

So Dick Davidson's hunch buys UP time. But the STB holds him to his word. It schedules another hearing on December 3, to see how matters are progressing. And if they aren't . . .

> Do not let any UP crews sit around waiting for a ride if they request one. This business of "you are not my crew" has got to stop. All crews are UP crews, so we must handle them as such.
>
> SP corridor director's report, Harriman Dispatching Center,
> October 21, 1997

History tells us this about megameltdowns: they all work themselves out. BNSF's Krebs told managers on October 21 their railroad has "the chance of a lifetime" to increase market share. The previous four weeks BNSF car loadings rose 10 percent from a year earlier; UP's fell 10 percent. "I know how tough it is to handle this now," Krebs said, "but we are [running] hours late instead of days late. Almost four hundred new locomotives due in 1998 will allow UP to handle 5 percent more business."

CSX and Norfolk Southern look on with sinking hearts. Their proposal to buy and divide Conrail between them is before the Surface Transportation Board. CSX and NS are singing a song called "We're Not UP, Conrail's Not SP" to anyone who will listen. But already

some important shipper groups, including chemical and plastics man-
ufacturers, oppose the filleting of Conrail. Should the STB approve
the purchase, look for the agency to require merger-implementation
reports from the buyers almost hourly.

But the real cipher is Union Pacific. Replacing SP people with UP
people in key jobs in Houston, it imposed Union Pacific's methods
on Southern Pacific's fickle terminal—so much for Davidson's claim
that his problems are "not merger related." Aside from Port Terminal
run-through trains, the service recovery plan envisioned no changes
whatever in Houston terminal operations. In other words, it's Hail
Mary, because Union Pacific remains determined to bend Englewood
to its will rather than design operations around what the yard can
accomplish.

The story making its way around in early November was that FRA
inspectors auditing UP safety practices now carry marketing and finance textbooks with them, in addition to the operating rulebooks.
Don't get it? Hey, it *is* a joke. But come December and January, if the
railroad can't demonstrate that its house is in order, the odds of forceful
government intervention will rise sharply.

January 1998 Trains

INDEX

Journalist FRED FRAILEY has written for *Trains* magazine for more than 40 years. He has authored five other railroad books, including *Twilight of the Great Trains, Southern Pacific's Blue Streak Merchandise,* and *Rolling Thunder* (with Gary Benson).

CPSIA information can be obtained
at www.ICGtesting.com
Printed in the USA
LVHW071815090720
659994LV00042B/488